Plant Dreaming Deep

Books by May Sarton

Plant Dreaming
Deep

By May Sarton

W · W · NORTON & COMPANY · INC · *New York*

Frontispiece photograph by Lotte Jacobi

FOR JUDY, *who believed in the adventure from the start*

CONTENTS

Happy the man who can long roaming reap,
Like old Ulysses when he shaped his course
Homeward at last toward the native source,
Seasoned and stretched to plant his dreaming deep.

—MAY SARTON, *after Du Bellay*

Plant Dreaming Deep

PROLOGUE

The Ancestor Comes Home

I HAD LIVED MY WAY into all this house is and holds for me for eight years before I brought "the ancestor" home. As I stood on a stool and hammered in a hook strong enough to support the plain, heavy oak frame and the portrait itself, I knew I was performing a symbolic act, and this is the way it has been from the beginning, so that everything I do here reverberates, and if, out of fatigue or not paying attention, I strike a false note, it hurts the house and the mystique by which I live. But now, as I lifted the frame and set Duvet de la Tour in his place, it was on a note of triumph, as if a piece of music where many themes have been woven together was just coming to a satisfying close.

"Well, old boy, here we are!"

He had been a long time coming through the centuries and

Photograph by Eleanor Blair

across the ocean from Normandy; I had been a long time growing up in Europe and America. Now fifty-four years old and the
last of my family, I stood on the yellow floor of the big room
and looked up at this presence from the eighteenth century: red
coat, curled white wig, and shrewd Norman face. Just above him
to the left is his crest, the tower of his name, "de la Tour." I
have always been amused by his name, such a romantic name
for such a commonsensical old boy. It too has its reverberations.
There is a charm in the contrast between "Duvet," which means
"down" as in "swan's-down," and that stubby, firm little tower.
The name suggests gentleness and strength; I savor it, and think
it suits this house, which has been as comforting as swan's-down,
a soft nest in time of trouble, and has been also a strong tower, a
defense against the world.

The portrait hangs over a Flemish chest of drawers such as
might have stood in his own manor house in Noordpeene, and
he looks perfectly at home, so much so that after that first day I
was hardly aware of his presence. He might always have been
here, looking down on me with a shade of amusement, and reminding me that if my head is in the clouds I had better be sure
my feet are firmly planted on the earth.

It amuses me, too, to realize that he died so far away in
about the year this house was being built in the village of Nelson, New Hampshire. By 1803 Duvet de la Tour was ending a
very long life. Born in 1700, his greatest ambition must have
been to live, as he did, through the eighteenth century and into
the dawn of the nineteenth, and so achieve fame as "the man of
three centuries." That epithet is all I know about him, except
that when asked how he managed to live so long he answered,
"Half a pint of applejack with half a loaf of bread for my breakfast each morning." (I plan to embark on this regime myself
after my ninetieth year.)

There are no facts to go by, but his life is clearly written in
his shrewd, humorous, reasonable face. Of course he would be
horrified by the ragged New Hampshire landscape outside, the
excrescences of granite that lie like huge beasts in my untilled

fields, the scrubby second growth of my woods which, since they were lumbered off years ago, serve only as shelter for deer, woodcock, raccoons, and foxes. Nor would he approve of my garden of English herbaceous borders, a disorderly tangle compared to the stiff parterres he must have laid out at Noordpeene. But he would approve of the weathered barn, full, now late in August, of new-mown hay, even though that hay is not for my cows but for those of the neighbors who cut it for me. He would approve of the character of the people who have lived here in Nelson since the late 1700's, for they too have had to be shrewd, stubborn, streaked with humor and pride, in order to survive— and some of them would not deny the validity of his receipt for a long life!

My parents always spoke of Duvet de la Tour as *the* ancestor, as if there had been no others, because he is the only one of whom a portrait exists. *The* ancestor he may be, but there is an English forebear whose disembodied presence I sometimes evoke, for I do have the story of his life, a charming little book published in London in 1805. John Elwes was an almost exact contemporary of Duvet de la Tour's, though he did not live so long, and for a very good reason. He was a miser, even a renowned one, for legend has it that he starved himself to death. At the same time this curious man was sometimes extravagantly generous, as on one occasion when he paid out thousands of pounds to release a friend from bondage and make it possible for him to marry. He was a true English eccentric, at the opposite pole from the French man of reason, and I find him most endearing. Let his biographer testify. Edward Topham says of him:

"He had the most gallant disregard of his own person, and all care about himself, I ever witnessed in man. The instances in younger life, in the most imminent personal hazard, are innumerable; but when age had despoiled him of his activity, and might have rendered care and attention about himself natural, he knew not what they were: he wished no one to assist him— 'He was as young as ever—he could walk—he could ride—and he could dance—and he hoped he should not give trouble, even when he was old.'

"He was at that time *seventy-five*.

"As an illustration of this, an anecdote, however trivial, may be pardoned. He was at this time seventy-three, and he would walk out a-shooting with me, to see whether a pointer I at that time valued much was as good a dog as some he had had in the time of Sir Harvey. After walking for some hours, much unfatigued, he determined against the dog, but with all due ceremony. A gentleman who was out with us, and who was a very indifferent shot, by firing at random, lodged two pellets in the cheek of Mr. Elwes, who stood by me at the time. The blood appeared, and the shot certainly gave him pain; but when the gentleman came to make his apology and profess his sorrow— 'My dear sir,' said the old man, 'I give you joy on your improvement—I knew you would hit something by and by.'

"In this part of his character, nothing could be more pleasant than was Mr. Elwes; it was the pecuniary part which ruined, as the Dramatist would say, 'the stage effect of the whole thing.'

"It is curious to remark how he contrived to mingle small attempts at saving with objects of the most unbounded dissipation. After sitting up a whole night at play for thousands, with the most fashionable and profligate men of the time, amidst splendid rooms, gilt sofas, wax-lights, and waiters attendant upon his call, he would walk out about four in the morning, *not* toward home, but into Smithfield to meet his own cattle, which were coming to market from Thaydon Hall, a farm of his in Essex. There would this same man, forgetful of the scenes he had just left, stand in the cold or rain, bartering with a carcass-butcher *for a shilling!*"

Later on, John Elwes spent twelve years in the House of Commons. "It is to his honor," his biographer tells me, "that in every part of his conduct, and in every vote he gave, he proved himself to be what he truly was, an *independent* country gentleman."

But of course what makes John Elwes haunting is "that strange *anxiety* and *continued irritation* about his money, . . .

the *insanity of saving*," as Edward Topham puts it. I recognize well the anxiety mentioned here. The only time that I, this remote descendant, made any real money in that form of gambling called "writing for a living," I felt compelled to give it all away, or spent it foolishly on machines that were supposed to save time but gave me endless trouble—an electric typewriter that went on buzzing in a nerve-racking way when I stopped to think, a primitive washing machine that inundated the bathroom floor and turned the simple matter of washing clothes into an ordeal. For me, "the irritation" of having money has always ended in the "insanity" of *not* saving, but mine is no doubt only a different way of reacting to the same psychological characteristic.

John Elwes would have felt more at home in a remote New Hampshire village even than Duvet de la Tour. He would have highly approved Yankee thrift and Yankee sobriety, as well as the Yankee extravagance exemplified by those legendary Boston ladies who "have hats" rather than buy them but give millions to hospitals, symphony orchestras, and the founding of colleges for the underprivileged.

I enjoy beginning this chronicle with an evocation of two ancestors because in this house all the threads I hold in my hands have at last been woven together into a whole—the threads of the English and Belgian families from which I spring (Flanders and Suffolk), the threads of my own wanderings in Europe and in the United States, and those shining threads, the values willed to me by two remarkable parents. Here they all weave their way into a single unfolding and unifying design.

And thereby hangs this tale. Let us begin at the beginning.

"To every thing there is a season, and a time to every purpose under Heaven." For forty-five years or so, I lived very happily without owning property, and in fact would have considered the owning of property a definite hazard. I felt then no responsibility except to a talent. I wandered, borrowing other people's lives, other people's families, with the nostalgia of the only child; and for many years could not decide whether I was a European or an American at heart. As for roots, they were there in my parents' house in Cambridge, on Channing Place, where the Flemish chests, my mother's desk, and the big *bahut* with its pillars of glowing walnut seemed to have found a permanent home. There my mother's garden grew and flowered and expanded. "Colonial expansion" she called it when she took over the end of the road, which did not really belong to us, to capture one flower bed with full sun on it! There my father added bookcases and record shelves as his libraries of books and records grew. It was inconceivable that those two vibrant personalities would both die comparatively young and that house have to be sold. It was the place I could always come back to from my adventures.

Those years between my twenty-sixth (when my first book of poems came out) and my forty-sixth (when I came to Nelson) *were* adventurous because, luckily for me, I had to earn my living. I am sure it is a good thing for a writer in the formative years to be forced out into the world from his self-enclosed preoccupations and anxieties. It happened that I was good at lecturing, partly because I had been schooled in the theater to project to an audience, to use my voice well, and not to be afraid of public appearances.

When I made the first of many lecture trips, in 1939–1940, I was unknown, the former director of an off-Broadway theater that had failed during the Depression, the author of a slim volume of poems and of one novel. The lecture circuit for poets had not yet become the big business it is now. I simply wrote to fifty colleges and offered to read for twenty-five dollars if they would put me up for a few days, and before I knew it I was beginning to plan and pin-point twenty or more such visits scattered all the way from Sterling, Kansas, to New Orleans, and from Charleston, South Carolina, to Santa Fe, New Mexico. My father came forward with a new Mercury convertible and the promise of fifty dollars a month to help me along, and I set out alone on an autumn, winter, and spring of unhurried exploration.

There were considerable gaps between engagements when my funds ran low, but then I holed in somewhere and wrote poems—ten unforgettable days in Eureka Springs, Arkansas; three weeks in New Orleans, where I managed to find a boardinghouse for eleven dollars a week, meals included. The whole trip was not at all what a lecture trip usually is, a hurried kaleidoscope of places and people, but rather a leisurely odyssey, the discovery of my America. I was always looking for the humanizing and illuminating perception of writers and poets about these landscapes I was seeing for the first time, and was amazed at how much has not yet been celebrated. Where is the poet of the secret wild Arkansas valleys? Of the great golden empty Texas plains? Of the Delta?

For me, the place of the greatest intensity turned out to be New Mexico, around Santa Fe, where I spent two months. The austere landscape, the great sunlit plateau dominated by the Sangre de Cristo Mountains, the "leopard land" dotted with piñon, affected me deeply. I had found one of the places on earth where any sensitive being feels exposed to powerful invisible forces and himself suddenly naked and attacked on every side by air, light, space—all that brings the soul close to the surface. There the poems flowed out.

Later on I was alone for days in Charleston, where I felt sharply, and for the first time, how in these United States a whole way of life may come and go in the space of fifty years —as in Charleston where rice built those exquisite plantation houses, then left them abandoned; as here in New Hampshire where Australian wool knocked out the sheep, and the painfully cleared fields went back to second growth. But in Santa Fe time is not that shallow. There one can go deep into a continuity as the pueblos and the culture they represent take one back at least eight hundred years through a single Indian dance. For a European that continuity is life-giving.

I came home from that trip not only enriched in every way as an American but with the good will of a nucleus of college presidents who have since asked me to return over and over again. That initial adventure has brought me many more. Through it I became the inhabitant of a continent and not just a refugee from Europe in a tiny corner of it.

But entering deeply into the life of a college for a few days and then moving on, or spending a week in a boardinghouse in a strange city is not the same as *living* somewhere, and what I meant by "life" was still rooted in Europe. During those years I went back whenever I could to the strong ties in England, France, Belgium, and Switzerland. I had not yet cut the umbilical cord.

> "I too have known the inward disturbance of exile,
> The great peril of being at home nowhere,
> The dispersed center, the dividing love;
> Not here, nor there, leaping across ocean,
> Turning, returning to each strong allegiance;
> American, but with this difference—parting."

That stanza of a poem called "From All Our Journeys" was written in the 1940's. But then, while my parents were still living, I could come back "from all the journeys" to Channing Place.

My mother died first, in 1950, after a long illness; we had watched that radiant being slowly extinguished, and there was relief at the end. My father fell like a great oak, dying in a few minutes of a heart attack. Early in the morning of March 22, 1956, he had been on his way to give a lecture in Montreal, but felt so ill that he turned back in the taxi from the airport. He died at home, the faithful Julia, his housekeeper, at his side. A half hour later the phone rang for me in Denton, Texas, where I was to have lectured that morning, and I flew back through that long day to a house that was no longer home. It was all sudden, violent, and terrible. Within a week the house had been sold, and within two months dismantled, the books gone, everything torn apart of the fabric of my parents' lives together. I went through those months like a person in a dream, hardly conscious, making decisions because they had to be made.

One of these decisions had to do with the old pieces of Flemish furniture, which I could not bring myself to sell, which I could nevertheless hardly keep for I shared a small house with a friend of many years and there was scarcely room for what we already possessed. Finally a temporary solution was found: the new owners kindly allowed me to store in the cellar at Channing Place my mother's desk with its many pigeonholes and secret drawers, the *bahut,* the long refectory table that matched it, and two eighteenth-century chests of drawers. They had survived the '14–'18 war, four long years, in the house in Wondelgem, in Belgium, while advancing and retreating armies bivouacked there; they had survived the ocean-crossing, and had moved with us from apartment to apartment until at last my parents owned their own house. Would these great pieces of our lives now rot in that cellar, unloved, uncherished, like so much old lumber? After a year they began to haunt me as if they were animals kept underground and dying of neglect. How long would they stay alive? And how long would the life in me stay alive if it did not find new roots?

I behaved like a starving man who knows there is food somewhere if he can only find it. I did not reason anything out. I did not reason that part of the food I needed was to become a member of a community richer and more various, humanly speaking, than the academic world of Cambridge could provide: the hunger of the novelist. I did not reason that part of the nourishment I craved was all the natural world can give—a garden, woods, fields, brooks, birds: the hunger of the poet. I did not reason that the time had come when I needed a house of my own, a nest of my own making: the hunger of the woman. I only knew that the old Belgian furniture must be rescued from that cellar.

If "home" can be anywhere, how is one to look for it, where is one to find it? For me, there was no ancestral "connection" that might have drawn me here or there, no magnet that might have narrowed down the possible choices. I could settle anywhere within a wide perimeter of Cambridge, for I intended to keep what I would not part with, my life with Judy, my place in her house, and the friends of many years.

People, meanwhile, began to advise me not to buy anything, warning me of what responsibilities and drains both on money and strength I would get myself in for, although Judy, from the first word about my dreams, gave unstinted support. Nevertheless, I began to wonder whether it was all madness, whether I had better stay as I was, give up the whole wild idea.

Everything in us presses toward decision, even toward the wrong decision, just to be free of the anxiety that precedes any big step in life. I was not wrong in divining that for me, if I took it, this step would mean radical change and so might be compared to marriage. No woman in her forties can afford to marry the wrong person or the wrong house in the wrong place! So I groaned and teetered and waited for life itself to make some sign. Not since the failure of the Apprentice Theatre twenty years before, and the decision then to put all my energy into becoming a writer, had there been such a frightening transition before me. I quailed.

But the guardian angel was not far off. He made his appearance, as he so often does, quite casually, at a luncheon with my friend Ray Baldwin. Ray listened to my lunatic complaints (I seem to remember bursting into tears over the cocktails) and asked, "Have you ever thought of looking in the Monadnock region?" Well, I had spent at least one summer in Dublin, but that was years ago in another life, for I had been there with the Apprentice Theatre for a summer of rehearsal before our first performances. No, I had not even thought of New Hampshire. I had thought I wanted to be near the sea.

A few days later I received a handwritten letter of some length, describing five houses in the Monadnock region that might be of interest. It came from Mrs. Rundlett, a real estate agent whom Ray Baldwin, acting quickly, had alerted. At the end of the letter I read these words: "Finally there is an eighteenth-century farmhouse in rather poor condition, with five fireplaces, and thirty acres of land, bounded by a brook. . . ."

Did the furniture in the cellar give a faint sigh as I read that memorable sentence? I know that I myself felt that prickling of the scalp that Emily Dickinson tells us is the sign of recognition before a true poem. Did the guardian angel gravely nod his head?

If so, why have I chosen to begin this book about a house and a village in New Hampshire by evoking an old Norman gentleman and an old English gentleman who would seem to have no visible connection with this part of the world?

Well, once an old lady in her late eighties walked into the big kitchen-living-room where "the ancestor" now hangs, looked about her, and asked in a rasping old-American voice, "Why do you have all this *Belgian* furniture in an old *American* house?"

I was too dismayed to answer. But I think this book is the answer, although she, brave soul, is dead and will never read it. The answer is, "Katherine Davis, I have brought all that I am and all that I came from here, and it is the marriage of all this with an old American house which gives the life here its quality for me. It is a strange marriage and its like does not exist anywhere else on earth . . . and just that has been the adventure."

ONE

I Meet My House

IT WAS A FINE May morning when we set out, Mrs. Rundlett and I and a friend of mine, to take a look at five houses. I do not have happy memories of that day; I was too anxious, and much of the time too depressed. The fact is that a house for sale has a slightly sinister atmosphere; life has gone stale in its abandoned shell. It happened that those we saw were far from each other, so that we trundled through unknown country for what seemed like hours, and I was over-aware of scrubby woods and sad stone walls with their silent testament to the fact that all this land had been cleared a hundred years or more ago and then grown back to jungle. One of the houses, it is true, was beautiful and stood in an open sunny meadow, but it was huge, still furnished, and smelled of other people's lives. Why had they left, I

Photograph by Lotte Jacobi

wondered? I had never hunted a house before and was unprepared for the shock of this public invasion of private atmospheres. By eleven o'clock I was almost ready to call off the whole thing, except that it did seem foolish not to take a look at the last house on the list, that dilapidated eighteenth-century farmhouse in the village of Nelson.

From Dublin we followed an interminable road through lonely woods for four miles, then emerged into a charming brick mill town sitting sedately beside a lake, and again veered off into thick woods. It began to feel like one of those journeys one takes in a dream, a journey that has no end, in search of something that can never be found, where if one wakes at last it is to the accelerated heartbeat of terror. I did not intend to live on the edge of nowhere.

But then, quite suddenly, the long road took an abrupt turn to the left and we found ourselves out in the sunlight of a small village green.

"This," Mrs. Rundlett said, "is Nelson."

I saw a tall white church with a tall white spire, a cluster of houses, an abandoned brick schoolhouse beside a clapboarded town hall, a tiny memorial library . . . and that was all. So silent, so serene, it felt as if we had just pushed a magic door open into the nineteenth century. There was not a soul to be seen.

Beyond the church we turned in under a stand of old maples, and there, a little back from the road, behind its semicircular drive, withdrawn from the village itself, stood the house. Still under the spell of so much light after so much darkness, I drank the sight in—first the pleated green fan over the white door, then the door itself, ample and welcoming, framed in two narrow windows, set off by delicate carved white pillars. I noted the wide granite step and the way it slipped into a grassy slope; the twelve-paned windows, the gently sloping roof above them, a chimney at each end. The whole impression was one of grace and light within a classic form, and I was so dazzled by this presence that for a moment I could only see, not hear. But then I heard it—an oriole, high up in one of the maples, singing his song of songs.

I had not heard an oriole since I was a child; in my agitated state these notes fell with an extraordinary resonance. I felt reassured. It seemed, in fact, like a sign. And then, as if woven through the song, I heard the silence. Each time I come back here the same miracle happens. I bring the world with me, but at a certain moment the world falls away and I am inside the life-restoring silence.

I shook myself free of the spell, and we went together to take a look at the realities—the tumble-down sheds that were pulling one end of the house askew, the ugly wreckage of an old barn left to rot where it had fallen, the unpainted back of the house. The word "dilapidated" began to loom rather large.

Though we had an appointment with the tenants, it took them a long time to answer our knock, and when they did, it was clear that they resented this invasion by prospective buyers, so our situation was awkward. Once more we were pushing in to an alien atmosphere; once more I felt ill at ease, swallowing the comments and questions I should have liked to make to Mrs. Rundlett. We went through the house in silence—through the low-ceilinged, dark kitchen, down a small dark passage to the privy, in bad condition. There was no running water, of course, only a rusty pump in the kitchen sink.

"There's a good well," Mrs. Rundlett said into the general gloom, "fed by three sources, I understand. It has never gone dry—built right into the back porch, you see."

Off the kitchen was a strange shallow room with a huge fireplace on one side. It was almost filled that day by a king-size, unmade bed. Here too we felt the cramp, as if we had entered the cave of shy wild animals. So it was a relief to emerge into the two front rooms, only one of them in use.

"A rare piece of luck to find five fireplaces and mantels intact," Mrs. Rundlett pointed out. "Usually in old houses they are boarded up. No one wants to keep five fireplaces going in winter when they can put in oil heaters."

My eyes rested on the lovely mantels, and on the moulding round the windows, and on the staircase with its elegant maple banister and thin white balusters. It was clear that the original builder had been a man of taste and an excellent craftsman, but these forlorn relics of his way with things seemed almost inappropriate to the house as it had become.

Only three of the five rooms downstairs were in use; upstairs all four were abandoned dumps of rubbish. Had I come too late? Could it still be brought back to life? Could the original builder's vision and style be resurrected through so much waste and the ravages of time and neglect? I felt a ray of hope—those mantels and moldings—but no conviction, no rising of the spirits such as had been induced by the oriole and the moment of rapt contemplation of the façade.

It was good to get out into the sunlight, the fresh May air, and to walk around the "new" barn at the back. "In good condition, as you see," Mrs. Rundlett reassured. What I saw was the lovely tobacco brown of the weathered boards, tobacco with a touch of lavender; what I saw was harness and other gear hanging inside as if someone had just put the horses out to pasture; and what I saw as I came out was the long meadow, an acre or so, rolling off toward woods and a gentle profile of hills, that necessary open space for the meditative eye. The barn and its surroundings felt alive.

Finally we got back into the car, and I took a last look at all that had quickened my heart at the beginning. Yes, it was beautiful. My mother would have felt its beauty deeply. But if I undertook to rehabilitate this derelict, I would have to do it alone. Did I have the courage to lift it out of its depression? The enormity of the undertaking lay heavy on my mind, so heavy that I did not even ask about the brook that day (it was nowhere in sight). My practical friend had grave doubts. She persuaded me at least to get some estimates from plumbers, carpenters, and a chimney man as to what it might cost to make the shell habitable, and Mrs. Rundlett agreed to do so and to let me know within a week.

So for a week I engaged in endless speculations and imaginings, trying to visualize not the present, but the past and the future. I was held by it, as one is held by a poem that has not

quite jelled, that haunts the nights. I had first to dream the
house alive inside myself. The most important thing was to make
light, air, space, within the dark cramped rooms. If I painted the
walls white, would that help? Would the dear Flemish furniture
ever fit into those spaces? Where would I sleep? Where would I
work? And if I could move out all that wreckage of the old barn,
would it be possible, maybe, to use the foundation as the wall of
a long perennial border? One thing was clear. I could very well
live in the five downstairs rooms and leave the second floor for a
later time. That would cut down on cost considerably.

It was a painful week, swung between doubt and hope. I
knew that tension well. It is just the same before I begin to write
a book or a poem. It is the tension of being on the brink of a
major commitment, and not being quite sure whether one has it
in one to carry it through—the stage where the impossible almost exactly balances the possible, and a thistledown may shift
the scales one way or the other.

At last the estimates came in: $800 for chimney work; $4000
for carpentry and general contracting work; $3000 for plumbing,
cesspool, bathroom, furnace. I could buy the place as it stood
(with thirty-six acres of woods and meadow) for $3900. That
made twelve thousand as a start, but everyone warned me that
these estimates were sure to be on the hopeful side.

In the end I knew I would have to trust to instinct, not estimates. Could I be happy in that house? Would poetry come
there? How could I know? I couldn't. What I came back to was
the structure: I had a solid, beautiful frame in which to create
something, if possible, worthy of it. What I came back to was
that moment of silence, and the oriole. Everything here has been
a matter of believing in intangibles, of watching for the signs, of
trying to be aware of unseen presences. In the end the oriole
tipped the scales.

On June 7th, 1958, I signed the deed and became the owner
of a broken-down house, a barn, and thirty-six acres in a remote
New Hampshire village—a village of which I knew absolutely
nothing.

TWO

Nest-Building

HAS ANYONE ever invested in a house and land whose ignorance was as total as mine? I knew absolutely nothing about houses, and next to nothing about country life. I had to depend on a stranger for the men I was hiring, sight unseen, but fortunately Mrs. Rundlett proved to be a wise and practical guide: she brought me Earle Naglie as general contractor. A wiry man with keen blue eyes and the gentlest manners, he must have realized at once that he had a tyro on his hands, and took me under his wing. I had, for instance, never heard of "sills," so I did not even know how lucky I was that the sills of my house were not rotten, and that the roof was good and solid.

I did have definite ideas of *what* I wanted done, but I hadn't the faintest idea *how* it was to be done. I wanted air, light, and

Photograph by Eleanor Blair

space. I wanted to keep everything that gave the house its dis-
tinction, the work of the original builder, but I had no intention
of making an historical reconstruction. I saw the house as becoming my own creation within a traditional frame, in much the
same way as a poet pours his vision of life into the traditional
form of the sonnet. Finally, I was determined to bring the old
furniture up from that cellar and into a warm shelter by October
first. What I told Earle Naglie was, in effect: "Keep costs down,
and get me in by October." If he was sometimes dismayed by
the impetuous, ignorant poet he had undertaken to work for he
did not show it.

We sat down together one June morning on the granite step
and drew up the big plans. I was rather reluctant to part with
the sheds, but Earle told me that it would be impossible to shore
them up. As it was, that whole end of the house had been pulled
so far askew that the kitchen felt rather like the deck of a ship in
a rough sea. Since the sheds would have to go, the possibility
opened up of making a new kitchen wall with place for a sink,
stove, frigidaire, and built-in cupboards and drawers—above all,
two small windows to let in some light. I vetoed traditional pine
paneling for the sake of white walls everywhere except in the
front hall. I had seen how splendid the old Spanish chests and
tables in Santa Fe looked against white adobe, and, besides making a good background for the Flemish furniture, white would
reflect all the light the house could hold. What color there was
would be paint on the floors—only one, in my study, was in
good enough condition to be sanded down and waxed. As in the
writing of a poem, ideas popped into my head as we went along,
and I suddenly remembered that I had been struck on our house-
hunting day by a mustard-yellow floor and how fine some rather
elegant old furniture looked standing on it. Why not a yellow
kitchen floor, a sour blue for the cabinets? Speaking in terms of
color made what we were doing seem real to me, and soon I was
beginning to tear out advertisements to show Earle the exact
blue and yellow I had in mind. The actual mixing and painting
was still months away, of course. And when the time came we

had to experiment a good deal before we could get the colors exactly right.

Color was my province, but everything else was in Earle's hands, from finding a space for a bathroom (he managed to squeeze one in behind the stairs) to making a new keyhole for the front door, to building a whole new end of the house, and (horrendous job!) getting rid of the privy at the back and carting off not only the sheds but the tons of rubbish that had collected beneath their shaky walls—those and hundreds of other jobs, small and big, which I do not even know about.

Considering how definite my ideas were, it must have seemed strange to the workmen that I did not hover over each stage of the transformation of this broken-down shell into a livable house. I suppose I came about five times during the summer to see how things were going. I was too ignorant to realize how many small decisions Earle had to make on his own because I was not there, and when I did come I was apt to have a new idea and ask casually for some apparently "little thing" which took time he had not counted on spending. But he was never discouraging, although he sometimes looked a little quizzical when I insisted "I have to move in in October, come what may!" He just smiled and said he would do his best.

Earle was an experienced and inventive contractor and carpenter and I had a pretty clear notion of what I wanted, but I know now that we would never have managed without the guardian angel. He was kept busy seeing to it that the right people turned up at the right moment. How often an unexpected visitor just "happened" to be there when a crucial decision had to be made! One day late in June it was Jeanne Taylor, a painter with a keen eye. She walked in, looked around, and said, "Why don't you knock out that wall between the kitchen and the back room and make one big kitchen-living-room out of it?" The minute she spoke I saw how genial an idea she had given us. The present partition contained a closet and a useless flight of back stairs; once it was taken down, we would have one splendid long room instead of two cramped ones, and the boxlike structure of the house would be opened up to a new amplitude and variety.

Earle sat down with his pad and pencil and made some calculations. The change would mean putting in a whole new forty-foot-long floor, for one thing, but he too saw that it must be done. "Never mind the cost," I said to myself, "that room will make the house," and so it has. The long floor still tilts slightly like the deck of a ship, a great place to walk up and down while thinking. What had been the cooking fireplace in the house (it still has a crane in it and ovens to one side) helps make a charming living end to the kitchen, instead of overheating the shallow little room it dominated before. There I can sit and read while something is cooking, or, when I have guests, still be part of the family while I stand at the stove. And the great yellow floor, twice as long as I had thought it would be, is an unending joy, especially in winter when even on a dark day I seem to be treading on sunlight.

Between visits of the guardian angel, the hard work went on, and once in a while I missed the heavenly hand. The hauling off of the fallen-in barn, a piece of work that had loomed large in my mind when I was making the decision to buy, proved to be quite simple and not expensive. The bulldozer is a great invention! It took just a few hours to clear the rubble away. But when I decided to get the loam from my own land to fill in what was to become a terraced garden in the foundations, there was no hand on my shoulder to warn me that my decision would make a garden full of rocks and stones on the one hand, and a sad pitted meadow on the other. I am still struggling with the former; nature is taking care of the latter, for already the naked places are covered with daisies and black-eyed Susans and wild strawberries. Nevertheless it was a mistake.

Then one day quite late in the summer Earle said to me, "About time you told me about that kitchen wall."

I had some ideas, but they were rather vague. We had pretty well cleared away what remained here of the life of Dr. Rand, the first owner, when we tore out the sheds, including the one where his boy had slept next to the barn, ready to leap up and harness the horses while the doctor dressed if a call came late at night. But I had begged Earle to hang onto two sets of square stubby drawers where medicines had been stored. I wanted to build those in. I wanted to keep something here of Dr. Rand's presence, in case a friendly ghost came back looking for home.

I felt a slight panic coming on about that wall, when Don Jasinski, an architect, just "happened" to walk in. He was the last person I expected to see, and he has never been back. But he had clearly got the message. I have not come to the conclusion that there is a guardian angel without considerable evidence!

Don looked around for some time, and I well remember the total concentration of that look. We were all silenced by it. Then he sat down on a pile of lumber and, with a stubby pencil, sketched out the kitchen wall on an old envelope. He set four little drawers in horizontally, to hold silver, dish towels, and odds and ends, and three vertically to one side of the stove. Then, keeping to the odd square shape of the drawers, he invented cupboards under the sink and over the stove and frigidaire. How easy it looked when it was done! And how well the design has served me! Within an hour Don was on his way, called no doubt somewhere else by someone else's guardian angel.

Five men worked under Earle Naglie's quiet direction, and I learned from all of them. They were my first real contact with life as it would be lived here. There was Tink, for instance, with his pointed head and bright eyes, who looked like an elf. Once when we were eating lunch, sitting around in a chaos of loose boards and tools, Tink told me about the spring, how long it takes to come, how long I would have to wait before I heard the peepers, and the thrill it is when that slight airy singing starts up at last. Good Heavens, I had no idea then what a peeper was! The workmen were all gentle people, just as curious about me, this odd fish who was moving into an old house alone to write, as I was about them. And I was learning from them, through my skin, without being really conscious of it, the perfect courtesy of the New Englander, a courtesy born of his own sense of equality

with anyone and everyone, rich or poor. I found myself talking
not only about sheet rock for the walls but about my own work,
as simply as if we were old friends. The fact is, of course, that a
writer feels much closer to any craftsman, to a farmer or carpenter, to anyone who works with his hands, than he does to
clerks or accountants. There is a real affinity between people
who make something, as I had learned years before when I felt
the same warm communion with the *vignerons* in the Touraine.

There was only one workman whom I never saw, because I
was away during the week he was here—the chimney man. I
heard about the fearful rats' nests he had had to dig out; he did
a good job of making all five fireplaces workable—in fact, the
draught is so good that I hardly need kindling—but he was not
an artist, and I have paid for my absence at a crucial time ever
since. The new bricks have been set in with too wide an inter-
stice of cement, and make a jarring sight under the beautifully
carved mantels. Luckily I am not a perfectionist about some
things, and at first I was so happy lighting wood fires everywhere that I hardly noticed the poor workmanship.

The reader must remember that the climate of New England
is phenomenally various, the temperature in a single year running anywhere from over 100° to minus 30°, so a livable house
has to be snug, and one must be able to depend on the ma-
chinery working through blizzards, extreme heat, sharp freezes,
and God knows what hazards and pressures. Now that the frame
of the house was standing at last, it was time to call in the expert
who would be busy under the floors and in the cellar, putting in
sewage pipes, a furnace, running water in the kitchen and bathroom, and a cesspool out near the barn. I had been lucky in my
contractor, and was equally so in Beland Peirce of the firm that
bears his name. Beland, who is a good deal younger than I am,
took a fatherly interest in my problems and did a superb job for
me. Although so efficient and high-powered, he appreciates the
eccentric, and respects the person who wants to save where it is
possible. When I asked him whether he could possibly find for
me an old-fashioned tub on legs (for I dislike those slippery low

modern bathtubs), he smiled an amused smile and suggested that I come down to the store and he would see what he could do. There I found an Aladdin's cave of ancient appliances of all kinds—not only just the tub I wanted, for a song, but, even better, a secondhand stove and a secondhand frigidaire. John Elwes would have been in Heaven!

It is not necessarily true in New England, despite the legend, that all workmen and contractors are honest, or temper the wind to the shorn lamb. But it is a fact that no one who worked on rebuilding this house took advantage of my ignorance in any way. When, as the years went on, I did occasionally get badly rooked by one workman or another, I looked back to the first days with a shiver of relief, a kind of apprehension in reverse, to think what might have happened had I fallen among thieves instead of among my good friends Earle Naglie and Beland Peirce.

By September it really looked as if I might be able to move in on schedule. I'm sure Earle had moments of doubt, and the last weeks were pretty active and tense, as I came in and out to measure and re-measure just where the furniture would go, to help mix the paint, to bring rolls of wallpaper for the hall. There was no time now to sit and eat a leisurely lunch and talk of peepers! I walked around with a pad and pencil, making lists of absolute necessities, then dashed back to Cambridge to buy beds, kettles, blankets, towels, lamps, end tables, the hundred and one things one has to think of when moving into a cold empty house. When it came to beautiful objects, I had inherited a rich store from Channing Place; but I was rather weak on ordinary useful things, like a toaster or a laundry basket.

At this point the miracle of friendship, which has come to renew the mystique of the house so many times since, began to manifest itself. My friends realized that my whole relation to the place was a little like that of an old maid who suddenly gets married. And pieces of their lives began to come to me to share in the adventure. So Rosalind Greene gave me her mother's old wing chair to set beside the fireplace, and she and her daughter Katrine had it re-covered for me. At that time I did not have a single comfortable chair and had decided that I could not afford to buy one, but I had dreamed of a wing chair, and here it was, wafted to me on the wings of love.

With that blessed chair came three objects to set about the fireplace, objects that spoke to me vividly of childhood summers I had spent under the wing of the Greenes at their River Houslin, set above the salt marshes of Rowley, Massachusetts. That house no longer exists, pushed aside by a new road, but here at Nelson the Hessians with their ineffable smiles support the big logs from my woods; the five-foot-tall flat shovel takes out ash to lay around my rosebushes in spring; and the little low bench where we all sat as children is there before the fire . . . waiting for Katrine, who always sat down on it at once, stretching out her long legs, whenever she came to stay. Katrine has died since I came here, so she is one of the presences who come and go at this strange intersection where I do not live in time, but where past and future flow together into the present as gently as the currents of air that sometimes make the curtains stir as if a hand just touched them.

But in September of 1958 I was much too anxious about immediate practical problems to think of anything else. For the final month I behaved like a hen trying to gather together a thousand chickens, for every time I drove up from Cambridge with a load I discovered some obvious lack I had never even imagined.

One day Earle and I suddenly realized that no plans for light over the sink and stove had been made. I dashed down to Sears Roebuck in Keene for long fluorescent lights—just in time for him still to be able to mask them before he began to paint the cupboards. When the bathtub and washbowl had been installed, it occurred to me that towels do have to be hung, and that a mirror and medicine cabinet are not bad ideas in a bathroom!

But at last everything was in order, and I was able to tell George Gardiner that he could bring around a truck on October first as planned. Mr. Gardiner is a Cambridge institution, a Negro who began as handyman and gardener, but has long since become an entrepreneur with trucks and men at his command. I had not expected him to come along himself, but he said, "I wouldn't think of letting your father's furniture go up alone, Miss Sarton. I'll be there to watch out for it. Besides, I want to see that house of yours!"

So a little touch from the past, from dear Channing Place, would be with me on the tremendous day.

THREE

Moving In

I HAD WANTED to move in alone, the house and I confronting each other at last with no one at all to intercede, on what I had imagined as a golden October day. Instead I walked into the chill emptiness in dark heavy pouring rain. I paced the painted floors and listened to the rain pelting the windows, and when I stopped walking, the silence—but for that sound—was so immense that I held my breath as if I were drowning in it. The rooms with no furniture to warm them felt too naked, and the white walls on which no paintings hung looked like hospital walls. Would the house turn out to be a lunatic asylum for a single lunatic?

It was a strange hour I spent there, a kind of limbo. I suppose I must have brought food and drink with me, but I have no

Photograph by Lotte Jacobi

memory of stowing it away. I had brought suitcases of clothes, a few boxes of china and a few paintings, but I was not ready yet to unpack. These things and I stood around and waited. The rain poured down. The hour became a lifetime of suspense. For the last time I wondered whether I had made a crazy decision, taken on more than I could cope with, whether I had the inner resources to live here at all, whether it would turn out to be a disastrous escape into nowhere.

And then, at last, at eleven, on the dot, the big truck drove in. George Gardiner directed the driver to back up right to the front door, so careful and tender toward the precious furniture inside that nothing even got wet. The curtain was going up on a play long held in the heart, at last being acted out. I was no longer afraid as, one after another, the heavy, awkward Flemish pieces were hauled in and fitted exactly, each into the space I had planned for it—my mother's desk with its many pigeonholes, and the high stool where she sat to write letters, beside the fireplace in the small room that I had come to call "the cosy room"; the huge *bahut* opposite the kitchen door on the yellow floor; the chest of drawers where I keep linen set in beside the kitchen fireplace; and the long refectory table under the two windows opposite. Finally the wing chair settled into its place by the fire, commanding that whole room. The miracle for me was that all these pieces suddenly looked as if they had always been exactly where they were now.

"Oh, Mr. Gardiner, it's beautiful!"

"You have a nice little place here, Miss Sarton. You really do."

He stood there in his overcoat, smiling a quiet smile, bringing me the thread of continuity I needed so badly between my parents' house and this one on this perilous day.

Now the last and most precious piece of furniture was carefully lifted out and set in my study, a closed desk with wreaths of flowers inlaid in its silvery-gray doors, a desk designed by my mother, much too elegant really for any house of ours, early modern with a definitely Japanese air. It had been designed as part of a suite that was to have been exhibited in Brussels in August 1914. Instead, it spent years in a warehouse, to be rescued finally and brought over to my mother as a surprise from my father, when they were still very poor indeed. As furniture goes, it is a jewel, the only jewel he ever gave her but far more alive than any precious stone could ever be. When it entered my house, the seal was set. The past, my own past, had gently moved in to take its place within that other past, the past of the house, about which I then knew next to nothing. I only knew that I felt welcomed, not rejected, that if I moved among ghosts they were good ghosts. And in that intuition I was not wrong.

As soon as George Gardiner left, I began to take possession in the way one can do only when the lares and penates are present and can make their blessing. My first thought was to hang two Japanese prints over the big fireplace and over the refectory table opposite it, a Hokusai and a Hiroshige—the first a fisherman casting his net at dawn in the presence of Fujiyama, the other a burst of fireworks in a night sky over a bridge and a cluster of little boats. I had imagined the big room as one that must hold some echo of the sea . . . here the house feels most like a ship, for a reason—the slight tilt of the floor. New Englanders have always been ocean-bound, each old house holding memories of at least one seafarer. When the Hokusai was hung, I drew out three blue-and-white Chinese plates to set side by side, in Flemish fashion, at the other end of the mantelpiece. And under the Hiroshige I placed the deep-blue jug with an inset pattern of white flowers on its round sides, which my mother loved to use for flowers (it had come from Ghent). "There," I said as I planted it on the refectory table. "There."

The difference these few gestures had made was simply immense. The house had already begun to feel inhabited by all kinds of presences besides my own. My eyes rested on the Japanese prints. They had been given to me by Jean Dominique, as the poet Marie Closset had chosen to call herself, she of the huge gray eyes and birdlike head. On the back of the Hokusai are these words in her hand: "That fisherman on the point of a rock who draws up to him his heavy destiny from the depths of the foaming waves, the divine mountain his only witness—what grandeur in that space around him, so empty, and so alive!"

(Here too, under the shadow of Monadnock, a whole region is dominated by a sacred mountain, changing in every light, always a presence to be reckoned with as we come and go. I am glad I have no view of Monadnock from my house for I always come upon the great silhouette with a shock of surprise and a lifting of the heart; it can never be taken for granted.)

But of course the print means most of all the maker of it, Hokusai himself, that man of prodigious energy and prodigious humility who could say when he was seventy-five, "I have drawn things since I was six. All that I made before the age of sixty-five is not worth counting. At seventy-three I began to understand the true construction of animals, plants, trees, birds, fishes, and insects. At ninety I will enter into the secret of things. At a hundred and ten, everything—every dot, every dash—will live."

The three plates had made their way from China on camel back to Beirut to pay a student's years of learning at the university there, and had been brought home to Channing Place by my parents after a golden year they spent in Beirut when my father became a student again himself, to learn Arabic. For a moment I stood and looked around and listened to the hum I had created in the big room. Then I lifted out a blue wooden fish and set it up as the final piece of decoration on the mantelpiece, and with it Muriel Rukeyser, who gave it to me when we lived across the street from each other in New York, came in to stay.

I longed now to fill the whole shell of the house with murmurs such as these, and I went about it in a kind of lucid fever. Let the walls be inhabited and no longer stare out at me, too white! Let Elizabeth McClelland's lamp with its green shade be lit on my desk—and let there be a desk, for I had still to make it by fastening legs on a six-foot-long door!

But first Kobo Daïshi must find his place. This reproduction of the famous ninth-century Japanese painting of the child sitting on his lotus, hands folded in prayer, circled in a thin gold line, had been with us from our first tiny apartment in Cambridge when we moved there in 1917. He had been a familiar spirit through my childhood. Surely he would feel perfectly at home over mother's inlaid desk, the soft pinkish orange of his kimono melding with the inlaid flowers on its doors? He did, and for the last eight years he has looked down on me as I write and lift my eyes to rest now and then on that composed and composing presence.

I was troubled by what to hang in the space above the mantelpiece in my study—a wide empty space between wall-to-ceiling bookshelves that Earle had set in for me. On the chance, I had brought up a silk panel, turquoise damask, embroidered by my mother with a geometric design in blue and gold. That panel had never found a place on the walls at Channing Place, but both the shape and the color fitted perfectly in my study. It was, I saw when I had hung it experimentally, surely meant as a background for flowers, and so it became a kind of stage where the whole glorious sequence could be played out, from daffodils and tulips in May, to iris, and then to the great white peonies, the vivid blue delphinium, the long sequence of lilies, to end with chrysanthemums and asters in the fall. It is the *tokonoma* of the house, the sacred place where beauty is kept alive in memory of the dead.

Sunlight pours into my study from four windows. Year by year the turquoise silk has faded to a gentle watery blue, the brilliant embroidery has softened, and it is lovelier than ever. "We love the things we love for what they are," Robert Frost reminds us. And he means, I think, that we love them as they change —he is speaking in the poem of a brook gone dry—as well as for what they once were. My mother's face changed from that of an English beauty to that of a wrinkled old woman and never lost its sweetness. But the eyes did not change, those grave gray eyes that could suddenly twinkle with merriment, but through which fierce grief and tenderness flowed out toward a mouse rescued from the cat's jaws, toward the fallen bird with a broken wing, toward all living things including flowers and her husband and child. In exactly the way her creations have done—the inlaid desk, the embroidered panel—she grew old only to grow more beautiful, though changed.

I suddenly realized that what I had brought with me into the house, and the house itself, were making it possible for the first time since the death of my parents to evoke their joys. For the first time the joy that surrounds them in my mind could be rooted again, and had a place to root in. The long grief rose and melted away as I have so often seen mist do over my fields in the early morning.

If my mother's joys are vividly present in my study, I find my father's joys in the big room. Just over my head on the wall behind the wing chair when I sit there reading in the evening is an abstract design, black on white, flowing in great ripples. It is an inscription in Arabic, the opening of the Koran, "In the name of God, the merciful, the compassionate," and it hung over the door to my father's study, to remind anyone who entered there, whether he was conscious of it or not, that the scientist lives as close to Mystery as anyone. My father led as devoted and disciplined a life as any religious; for him the writing of the history of science was a vocation, and he served it through his whole life with the whole of himself. Whenever I choose to risk my vocation against any hope for security I cannot help but evoke George Sarton. What I see then is no stern father figure, but the great beaming smile with which he explained to mother and me some decision of his own that was sure to enrage the Establishment! He remained to the end something of a saint, and something of an *enfant terrible*. His stance was not always wise perhaps, but it was endearing.

So on that first day in this house I found the joys my parents had willed to me, and saw them take shape in concrete form on my white walls. These beautiful signs of a continuity almost erased the irony that without their early deaths I could never have invested in such a house at all, for I was able to do so only because of what I had inherited. But now I knew, in a way I had not before, that what I had inherited was life-giving and life-restoring, and would be so to the end of my life and perhaps beyond.

On that day, the first day here, I was glad to draw also on an American tradition, on something among the lares that came only from my own past, a delightful crayon of Lake Hoopatong, New Jersey, by Izrael Litvak, the primitive painter. It came to me through the enthusiasm of that most poetic and fervent of art dealers, J. B. Neuman. I can still remember how he spoke of Litvak, then quite unknown. "Look at that," J. B. said, his liquid eyes shining. "That man has never been inside a museum, has never seen a painting. Until he was seventy he was a cabinet-maker. Then, after he retired, he began to draw with crayons for his own pleasure. Isn't it wonderful? Look at it!" And the best of it all for J. B. was that this cabinetmaker from the Bronx had become a local hero. He rubbed his hands together with the joy of the whole thing, and it was part of his joy that the drawing would find its way into a poet's house. For years I used to send out a Christmas poem to my friends. J. B. was one of the few who always answered, and until just the other day I kept his last card on the mantel in my study. It said "Long live poetry!"

When the Litvak was safely hung over mother's desk in the cosy room, I had nearly reached the end of my strength. But I felt I must establish just one more presence, a seventeenth-century mirror in a plain wooden frame, which I set over a small chest of drawers that had gone unnoticed on the landing at Channing Place but lends quite an air to the cosy room. The mirror has always delighted me because whatever it reflects seems to sink down through layers and layers of time as through water, so one's own face becomes someone's face long ago, and the flowers I set there, especially peonies or shirley poppies, take on a magic solubility in the reflection as if they were floating away through time, as indeed they are.

I had just reached the loose end of exhaustion, and that little shiver of apprehension as the light goes, when I heard an exhilarating tinkle—the ancient front-door bell sounding for the first time. I had been living the last hours in the past. But this was the present. Who could my first guest be?

Once more the guardian angel had been at work, for it was Ray Baldwin! He told me that he had had business in Peterborough and thought he would drop in on his way home. Dear blessed man, without him this story would never even have begun! We raised a glass to the house, and to the future here—did he, I wonder, have doubts as to what it might be? It must have seemed rather lonely in the chill of evening. But at any rate he surely saw, and must have approved, the shine in my eyes. It was a different person from that despairing woman he had taken out to lunch only a few months before.

Finally at the end of that long, rainy, glorious day, I turned out the lights and fell into bed. At first there was too great a buzz of things still to be done in my head, but at last I could listen, first to the silence, and then, through it, to the infinite number of sounds an old house contains in the night. There were small creaks, a door opening in a draught, then the scurry of a field mouse somewhere in the kitchen, and something less tangible, as if things themselves breathed very softly, as if the old furniture were settling down. All these sounds together made the house feel like a ship. I did not know where the ship would take me, but I knew it was snug and beautiful, and I knew that its passenger was both inward and outward bound.

FOUR

With Solitude for My Domain

I WOKE TO SUNLIGHT, the washed crystal air after storm, the maples all lit up, translucent, a brilliant world of blue and gold, almost incredible after the darkness of the day before. I was learning right away the immense pleasure it is to have no idea what one will see on waking, so violent and unexpected are the changes in our weather here. I went from window to window, and stood for a moment behind my desk looking out at the sturdy white church and its strong steeple, standing high over the trees all around, so it seemed to float like a ship on their watery gold. The church stands across open meadow—*mine*, I thought, with a start of possessive pleasure. No one can ever come to break this open space, nor take from me the daily vision of so much power and so much promise just across the rough field.

Photograph by Eleanor Blair

The dreadful outer gloom of the day before served now to make more dazzling the beauty all around me.

Whatever I did not get done, I thought, I must go outdoors to explore. After all, there were more than thirty acres out there, and I had been only once to see the brook down through the second meadow and the ragged woods beyond, at the very border of the property. But when I did go out that day it was to make a quick dash to Peterborough to find rugs. I was wild to get settled as soon as possible, so that I could begin *living* in the house at last. And there was another reason for haste. I was to have just ten honeymoon days alone before my first guest was due to arrive, the dearest, the most unexpected guest I could have imagined.

Céline Limbosch had decided, in her mid-seventies, to embark on a freighter from Belgium to this new world for the sole purpose of seeing me in my house! "Aunty Lino," as I call her, was my mother's oldest friend, my closest tie to Europe, indeed "family." No one else alive remembers the house in Wondelgem where I was born; I suspect that she may have helped my parents choose the *bahut* when they were engaged to be married; at any rate I know that she held me in her arms on May 3rd, 1912, before my own mother did. I spent two separate years in Aunty Lino's house near Brussels when I was seven and fourteen, went to school with her children at the *Institut Belge de Culture française*—that was Marie Closset's school, she of the Japanese prints. Céline's husband, the poet Raymond Limbosch, had been a kind of father-in-poetry to me. And it was for their firm in Brussels, the *Arts Décoratifs,* that my mother had designed furniture, including the desk in my study. During the months when my mother lay dying, it had been hard to deny Céline's generous longing to come over and help us, but now at last I could welcome her with all my heart. Of all the people in the world she alone could recognize exactly what I was hoping to create here, would note every color, hear every reverberation, and fuse in her beautiful gesture my Europe and my America. She did not need to be summoned by the guardian angel—she came as a guardian angel herself.

But for the ten days before her arrival, I was, as I wished to be, alone.

During those ten days the only person I spoke to was Mr. Upton, the mailman, who drove up every morning at about eleven to deposit the mail in a row of wonderfully un-uniform mailboxes at the edge of the green. Horace Upton was then in his eighties, but he still went coon-hunting sometimes all night, and then drove his route as usual. I did not realize for months—so great is New England reticence—that my own post office was just two miles away at Munsonville on Granite Lake! For months I drove four miles late every morning to post my letters in the opposite direction. I did not even know that Mr. Upton collected outgoing mail every afternoon. I had to learn everything from the start, on my own, and that was part of the adventure.

It was what I had come for. Silence was the food I was after, silence and the country itself—trees, meadows, hills, the open sky. I had wanted air, light, and space, and now I saw that they were exactly what the house had to give. The light here is magic. Even after all these years, it still takes me by surprise, for it changes with every hour of the day and with every season. In those first days it was a perpetual revelation, as sunlight touched a bunch of flowers or a piece of furniture and then moved on. Early in the morning I watched it bring alive the bronzed-gray of the bird's-eye maple of mother's desk in my study and make the flowers in the wreaths suddenly glow. In the afternoon, when I lay down for an hour in the cosy room, I saw it dapple the white mantelpiece and flow in waves across the wall there. And when I went into the kitchen to make tea, there it was again, lying in long dazzling rectangles on the yellow floor. This flowing, changing light plays a constant silent fugue, but in those first days I had still to learn how different the music is as the seasons come and go. In January and February the light is brilliant as snow is reflected on the white walls. In summer the light turns green; the shadows become diffuse. This, my first experience of it, was in October of course, and in October one's eye is pulled outward, to look out and up into fiery bowers of maple leaves or, early in the morning, across frost-silvered meadows.

Inside and out I found myself in a world that kept me in a state of perpetual Mozartian joy. I can still remember the first time I witnessed the windows of the barn shining bright red in the afterglow, and the first time that same afterglow took the low hills all around the village so that, although we were already in darkness, we lay in a luminous purple bowl, and the first time I saw the church steeple spot-lit, dazzling white against dark wind clouds.

All those first days the light said, "Go outdoors!" But it also said, "Stay inside!" And ever since, I have been torn by all the lives I live here and the difficulty of choosing any one at any given moment. Those first days I often chose "inside"; the house had to be rebuilt first as a physical being—that job was now nearly accomplished—but just as important was the intangible structure, the way things chose to happen day by day, or the way I chose to make them happen, as I began, quite consciously, to build the metaphysical frame.

> "What I possessed was all my own,
> Yet not to be possessed at all;
> And not a house or even hearthstone,
> And never any sheltering wall.
>
> There solitude became my task,
> No shelter but a grave demand,
> And I must answer, never ask,
> Taking this bridegroom by the hand."

I knew, from having watched my father hack down the incredible amount of work he accomplished day by day and year by year, how supportive a routine is, how the spirit moves around freely in it as it does in a plain New England church. Routine is not a prison, but the way into freedom from time. The apparently measured time has immeasureable space within it, and in this it resembles music.

The routine I established in the first ten days has remained much the same. It revolves around the early morning hours at my desk, then moves gradually out into the rest of the house, as I lie down after lunch in the cosy room for an hour or two, and finally get up and, from May through November, go outdoors to garden for two or three hours before supper. In winter there are always indoor games to be played, such as doing a laundry or getting the files in order (a job that is never done!) or writing letters. I find that I must get up early, at six in summer, at half past six in winter when the morning star is still bright in the dark sky, or the best hours of the day get crowded in. I have to go to bed early if I am to have primary energy to call on for the morning's work, although I read two or three hours before I turn out the light.

I found out very soon that the house demanded certain things of me. Because the very shape of the windows has such good proportions, because the builder cared about form, because of all I brought with me, the house demands that everywhere the eye falls it fall on order and beauty. So, for instance, I discovered in the first days that it would be necessary to keep the kitchen counter free of dirty dishes, and that means washing up after each meal; that the big room is so glorious, and anyone in the house is so apt to go to the kitchen windows to look out at the garden or into the sunset, that it would be a shame to leave it cluttered up. The white walls are a marvelous background for flowers, and from the beginning I have considered flowers a necessity, quite as necessary as food. So from spring to late October I spend the hour just after breakfast in the garden, picking whatever I need to rearrange or start fresh six or more bunches. It is one of the best hours of the day, unless I am seriously tired; then it becomes, I must confess, a bit of an ordeal. But it is worth it even then, for wherever I look for the rest of the day there is always somewhere a shaft of light on flowers, and I feel them strongly as part of the whole *presence* of the house.

Choosing, defining, creating harmony, bringing that clarity

and shape that is rest and light out of disorder and confusion—
the work that I do at my desk is not unlike arranging flowers.
Only it is much harder to get started on writing something!
Teaching also is hard work, and probably (though in a different
way) as creative as writing is, but there is always the class there
to draw the best out of a teacher, so he does not have to make
the same huge effort to "connect with" the work at hand. The
writer, at his desk alone, must create his own momentum, draw
the enthusiasm up out of his own substance, not just once, when
he may feel inspired, but day after day when he often does not.
The teacher is supported also by what he teaches, whereas the
writer faces a daily battle with self-questioning, self-doubt, and
conflict about his own work. Half the time what he finds on his
desk in the morning looks hardly worth tinkering with; in the
cool morning light every weakness is exposed.

Every writer has his own ways of getting started, from sharp-
ening pencils to reading the Bible, to pacing the floor. I often
rinse out my mind by reading something, and I sometimes manage to put off getting down to the hard struggle for an uncon-
scionable time. Mostly I am helped through the barrier by
music. I play records while I am writing, and especially at the
start of each day one particular record that accompanies the
poem or chapter I am working at. During these last weeks it has
been a record by Albinoni for strings and organ. I do not always
play that key record, but it is there to draw on—the key to a certain piece of work, the key to that mood. The romantic compos-
ers, much as I enjoy listening to them at other times, are no
help. Bach, Mozart, Vivaldi—they are what I need—clarity and
structure.

Here again the house itself helps. From where I sit at my
desk I look through the front hall, with just a glimpse of staircase and white newel post, and through the warm colors of an
Oriental rug on the floor of the cosy room, to the long window at
the end that frames distant trees and sky from under the porch
roof where I have hung a feeder for woodpeckers and nuthatches. This sequence pleases my eye and draws it out in a kind

of geometric progression to open space. Indeed, it is just the way rooms open into each other that is one of the charms of the house, a seduction that can only be felt when one is alone here. People often imagine that I must be lonely. How can I explain? I want to say, "Oh no! You see the house is with me." And it is with me in this particular way, as both a demand and a support, only when I am alone here.

By eleven each morning it is time for a cup of coffee and to go out and taste the air, and to see what there may be to harvest from the mailbox on the green. The mail holds me by a thousand threads to all my lives in Europe and scattered over the United States. It reassures me that within the physical solitude of Nelson I am never alone in the world, and I can still hear all the voices and try to answer them, from the great world griefs— starvation in India, apartheid in South Africa, the plight of our own sharecroppers, the agony of the American Negro—to all the more personal joys and conflicts that fly through the air to reach this silent village. Of course I should have the strength of mind to wait till afternoon before I let all these reverberations begin. But that is a self-discipline I have not achieved. Life conspires against art (and maybe a good thing it does!). Without the daily mail I would become less than human. But even here the battle for time to work, and for the quiet state of mind that makes work possible, goes on day after day. I give myself an A on the rare morning when I am so absorbed that I do not lift my head and catch sight of the station wagon bearing the mail, as it flashes past.

In that first week, I felt I was running all the time. There were hundreds of things I had in mind to do, things about the house, things about the garden, besides the spate of poems that had been pushing their way out. But I imagined that, as time went on, this state of affairs would calm down and I myself would calm down, to lead the meditative life, the life of a Chinese philosopher, that my friends quite naturally imagine I must lead here, way off alone in a tiny village, with few interruptions and almost no responsibilities.

But in all the eight years I have lived here, it has not yet become a quiet life. It is life lived at a high pitch. One of the facts about solitude is that one becomes as alert as an animal to every change of mood in the skies, and to every sound. The thud of the first apple falling never fails to startle the wits out of me; there has been no sound like it for a year. Sometimes a log crumbles in the middle of the night with a soft explosion and wakes me out of sleep to wonder what is happening; and when the thermometer goes far below zero I have occasionally been terrified by what sounds like a pistol shot but is actually a nail popping out of a clapboard. The intense silence magnifies the slightest creak or whisper.

But more than any such purely physical reasons for staying on the *qui vive,* there are inner reasons for being highly tuned up when one lives alone. That alertness is also there toward the inner world, which is always close to the surface for me when I am here, so it may be a mouse in the wainscot that keeps me awake, but it may just as well be a half-formed idea. The climate of poetry is also the climate of anxiety. And if I inhabit the house, it also inhabits me, and sometimes I feel as if I myself were becoming an intersection for almost too many currents of too intense a nature.

People often ask me if I am not afraid, and I can honestly say that I have almost never been, except on one or two occasions when someone has rapped at the door late at night, usually someone who has lost his way. No, it is not fear, but an exceptional state of awareness that makes life here not exactly a rest.

Yet every day curves through the anxieties and oppressions and conflict of the morning to the joys of the afternoon toward the evening when time opens up and pressures let down. On those first autumn days, the dark was closing in by six. It was time to sit down in the wing chair by the fire and have a drink, read a little, think about supper. It was time to dream . . .

In that first week I established a rite about supper. When I sit down at the deal table, there are flowers; there is a bottle of wine, and the table has been carefully set as if by a good servant. There is a book open to read, the equivalent for the solitary of civilized conversation. Everything has been prepared as if for a guest, and I am the guest of the house.

FIVE

The House Opens Its Door

We DROVE UP FROM CAMBRIDGE, Céline and I, on the tenth of
October. I take that drive often and never tire of it, for it makes
a sampler of rural New England at its best. My route follows
back roads, through farmland and villages, much of it through
woods and open field; it passes Groton, surely one of the loveliest of towns, with its stately houses set back on immaculate
green lawns under the flowing fountains of wine-glass elms; and
finally it climbs over a steep range of hills before coming into
Peterborough. In October there are half a dozen roadside stands
on the way, rich cornucopias spilling out pumpkins, every kind
of squash, eggplants, lettuce, beets, carrots, and apples, with
bottles of cider arranged in neat rows along the edges. But
Céline was so full of her recent adventures and had so much she

Photograph by Eleanor Blair

must tell me, about the rough voyage, the landing in Baltimore, and all she had seen there and in Washington, that we flew past without really seeing any of the wonders. I did stop once to buy two huge pumpkins to set on the back porch as part of this housewarming, and to carve out later for Halloween. But Nelson was the magnet, and perhaps Céline was deliberately shutting out everything else to get the full impact there of her first sight of New England.

At last we turned into the village green, past the church, and up to the front door. While I unloaded, she sat down on the sill, the door open behind her, a glass of milk in her hand . . . and the silence fell at last, the silence of Nelson. I saw her look up at the astonishing gold of the maples, and across the green to the brick schoolhouse and the tiny library. We had arrived.

We had arrived through all the years, and the wars, and the deaths, through all the partings—when each time we thought we might never see each other again—through all the hopes and fears, to this moment of luminous quiet.

Only when it had been tasted to the full did she get up and come in to walk eagerly all around the house, to look at everything with murmurs of recognition, laying a hand gently on the *bahut,* picking up the blue jug and naming for me the pottery where it had been made two hundred years ago, half closing her eyes as she took in a perspective or a color, and finally saying what I had hoped to hear: "It is so like your mother—her taste, her sense of color—I see her everywhere! How she would have loved it, dearie!"

We had three days before the first guests were to arrive— Judy, who had not yet slept in the house, and Louise Bogan, the poet—three days of pure gold. Céline's intoxicating energy poured out in a hundred directions, noticing everything that needed to be done, making suggestions, and more often than not carrying them out herself before I knew what was happening. She had seen a long piece of granite lying at the edge of the rough grass which I called "the lawn." Why not bring it up and set it in below the granite step at the front door? "It would make a little more of an entrance, don't you think?" *That* she could not do herself, but it was her idea, and it looks exactly as she thought it would.

One of the passions Céline shared with my mother was the passion for gardening. Her own garden in Belgium, slowly created over forty years, is a series of bosks and bowers and long *allées*, of perennial borders and unexpected formal squares that one may come upon around a hedge; it contains a small orchard where the grass is kept cut under the trees, a pond for the ducks, a *potager* exactly like a child's drawing, so neat it is. Her garden is a poem, haunted still by her poet-husband.

> "I see it now, an illuminated page.
> The assiduous monk in his joy did not spare
> Costly vermillion and gold, nor the rich sage.
> He painted a garden as haunting as a prayer,
> Where children rest still in long revery.
> Stay, precious light, on the snow-white peony!"

If I evoke it here, it is because I have just come upon a snapshot taken of Céline with me in what was to become my garden. Céline is seated on a hideous pile of rubble and loose rocks with some ragged bushes behind her, and I stand at her side, smiling the smile of the triumphant owner of this Paradise! She never questioned what I saw in my mind's eye, and eagerly shared in the vision of "what might be" one day. She did more; she set to work at once with the old gardener's *expertise,* her beautiful small hands grasping a spade with a strength I could not command, and began to dig up and prepare one of the beds in front of the house. These were choked by weeds and a mixture of orange day lilies and pink, old-fashioned moss roses. Céline agreed with me that they did not go together, and we decided there and then to put the day lilies somewhere else. By the end of the morning I had been provided with a beautifully neat and deeply dug bed.

The next day a load of firewood was dumped in front of the porch. It seemed to me a herculean labor to stack it, but that indomitable woman took one look and said, "We'll do it now. Working together, it won't take us long." And indeed it was done in a couple of hours. There is something very satisfying about a well-stacked cord of wood on a back porch. It gave the house an air, I felt. Someone had moved in who meant business. We celebrated with a great fire in the big fireplace that evening, and talked and dreamed like two pioneers in a wilderness. For though the house itself was now restored to beauty and order, outside and all around there were still only rubble and weeds.

Our last day together was unexpectedly warm, so it was my turn to do the hard work while Céline, whose heart must be spared in hot weather, sat on a big stone, wearing her white sunbonnet (it makes her look like a character out of Beatrix Potter) to direct the operation. It was an important one, the first planting of perennials, phlox, and peonies, in what I hoped would become an herbaceous border against the foundation of the old barn. Céline provided an obbligato of Belgian exclamations, such as "Sapristi!" and "Saperlipoppette!" as she watched me dig in with a spade only to hit one rock after another. These had to be cajoled, attacked with a crowbar, and finally sucked out one by one like prehistoric teeth, while both she and I learned what it means to garden in New England. That backbreaking work is never done; the local joke has it that we *grow* rocks. Céline could not help me there, but it was a comfort to have her reassurance when I showed her the plants themselves, so dead and strange-looking in their cellophane bags, so unlike the glossy photographs that I had admired when I sent in the order.

"Just wait," she told me, "time and nature are very resourceful."

Then the weekend was upon us, and the first cherished guests. It was in every way an exceptional occasion, for I have never had so many sleeping under the roof since. I like to invite my friends one by one, so that the atmosphere is that of a *solitude à deux*.

With four of us together that first weekend, there was not much silence, and it all had a rather larky, improvised air, since

I did not yet even have a proper guest room or upstairs bathroom. When we finally got sorted out and on the way to bed, the fifth "person," our cat, refused to come in. Like all our cats, he had come to us as a foundling, a lanky cat with large green eyes and a very sweet disposition. His back was striped like that of any good tiger cat, but he had white arms, which made him look as if he had on long woolen underwear. We had named him Union Suit.

At about two in the morning Judy and I, who were sleeping in the unfinished bedroom upstairs, started up wide awake: we had both heard a startling sound outdoors. It was a loud yet muffled roar; it came from down in the woods below the garden; and Union Suit was out, and far too visible, in his whiteness, for his safety. So we pulled on coats and shoes and ran out into the frosty air. The sky was unbelievably brilliant with stars—stars so thick and so large that they looked like daisies. Could we have imagined that strange sound? No. There it was again, sending shivers down our backs . . . a muffled, angry bellow. It sounded like some primeval monster, not quite real, yet it was real. Had Union Suit heard it? Evidently, for in a few moments he came running in to our call like a small white ghost, and we went back to bed.

Céline was hugely amused by our tale the next morning, and, since she had been fast asleep, did not, I think, really believe us. But wilderness is close to the quiet village green . . . only the other day a black bear was seen at the crossroads a mile away, and last autumn a moose was reported by someone in a neighboring village. The hazard of the intense silence is that any sound becomes magnified; imaginary creatures are often abroad. Only last summer I woke after midnight, sure that a mysterious gathering of men were muttering in my field, but it turned out to be bullfrogs! The sound had been carried by the wind from at least half a mile away.

It seemed natural and good that the house was "warmed" by three people who represented three widely different areas in my life: Céline, who brought back my childhood and Europe; Judy, with whom I have shared everything (including a sequence of cats) for more than twenty years; and Louise, who exemplifies the life of poetry—for I had learned Louise's poems by heart long before I knew her, and when I first walked into her apartment high over the Hudson I was deeply moved, for it had an air, an atmosphere, very like Jean Dominique's study in Belgium. In each instance I walked into a room where I knew at once that much had been thought and felt, a room where books had souls, where life was lived at great intensity in the silence. So during those two happy days of the first October, a web of delicate threads between past and present was woven between my guests, and me, and the house.

When there are guests here, I do some things I never do when I am alone. One of them is to go for walks. When I am alone, there is so much else to do that I rarely venture down into the woods. Perhaps I am a little wary because it is easy to get lost there, and if I did get lost and broke a leg, it would not be a simple matter to get "found" again. So I was eager to walk the boundaries with these three friends.

It had looked like a pleasant woodsy walk, to follow an old stone wall down to the brook, there turn eastward along it, and come out eventually on a dirt road that would bring us back to the village. I had no idea what second growth is like, nor that I was leading my friends into a nerve-racking tussle with thick clumps of alders, with dark tangles of hemlock, in and out among monolithic rocks and patches of skirt-tearing blackberry bushes! When the stone wall crossed a dump, we had to trample our way through rusty tin cans. From time to time Céline and I stopped to answer faint cries of distress behind us, but at last we heard the reassuring sound of water and hallooed back that the ordeal was nearly over. In a moment we came out onto soft pine needles and saw the brook itself, tumbling over boulders, eddying around fallen trees, rippling over shingle, and pausing now and then in shallow brown pools . . . the brook was perfect.

When we had recovered from this expedition, with the help of a martini, some lunch, and a nap, I suggested a little drive.

An exploring drive is another of the joys that, like walking in the woods, I do not often indulge in when I am alone. It is a game to follow one of the innumerable dirt roads that lead out of the village to discover where it ends—at a deserted lumber camp or an abandoned farm, at a beautiful lake or halfway up a mountain—who knows? This time we were lucky in the season, for we wandered through a golden world. Once the car not only rolled under a magnificent stand of maples but on untrammeled fallen leaves, so that, with light over and under and all around us, we seemed to be in a tunnel of gold. We were also in luck because I had happened on a road that took us finally up to a great open perspective with Monadnock standing up at its most splendid to the south and the gentle hills of Vermont rolling away into a blue and purple distance to the north, the eye of a lake lighting the whole prospect up with its blue. Céline could hardly believe that within a mere two-hour drive from Boston we would find ourselves in such a rural and unspoiled world; it reminded her of the English Lake Country.

How brief yet how full that first encounter between my new life and its first guests! So much greater, then, the sense of absence when the house and I found ourselves alone together after they had gone. It was my first experience of the transition back to solitude, the moment of loneliness, the shadowy moment before I can resume my real life here. The metaphor that comes to mind is that of a sea anemone that has been wide open to the tide, and then slowly closes up again as the tide ebbs. For alone here, I must first give up the world and all its dear, tantalizing human questions, first close myself away, and then, and only then, open to that other tide, the inner life, the life of solitude, which rises very slowly until, like the anemone, I am open to receive whatever it may bring.

It does not always bring happiness, but it always brings life of a special kind. I have waited, sometimes for years, for someone who did not come, whether human or angel. But part of the quality of my life here has been in the waiting itself, as it was for my old friend S. S. Koteliansky, whose house in St. John's

Wood held as many reverberations for him as mine does for me. Katherine Mansfield had lived there—the pear tree in his garden was *the* pear tree of "Bliss"—and there Kot, that patient, impatient lover of writers, often waited as I have done, his wiry hair bristling, a Russian cigarette in his mouth, and a book open before him at the deal table where we sat so many hours drinking Russian tea and talking about everything under the sun. I had sensed about his house what I was coming to know about mine, and had set it down years ago.

> "If the house is clean and pure,
> Fiercely incorruptible,
> God is ever at the door,
> The Father and the Prodigal.
>
> Should He never be aware
> Of the order of each plate,
> Still they will be shining there
> And the floor immaculate.
>
> Though at times the things revolt,
> Fickle water or damp wall,
> The chipped cup or stiffened bolt
> (Love, where is your Prodigal?)
>
> Still the house waits and is glad;
> Every teacup makes a welcome,
> Every cup aspires to God
> Even if He never come.
>
> And whether He exists at all,
> The Father and the Prodigal,
> He is expected by these things,
> And each plate Hosannah sings!"

Solitude itself is a way of waiting for the inaudible and the invisible to make itself felt. And that is why solitude is never static and never hopeless. On the other hand, every friend who comes to stay enriches the solitude forever; presence, if it has been real presence, does not ever leave.

So Céline came, and went, but she is here, both tangibly and intangibly, for as long as I live. She is here in the garden she helped to make, in the woods we explored together, and she is here in another and more physical sense. For a drawing of her now hangs over the mantelpiece in the cosy room. Her arms are folded in calm possession of herself and the world around her; her glasses have slid halfway down her nose, and she meditates not on what her eyes see but on what they cannot see. She looks as if she belonged here. Someone who looked up at her face, ignorant of who she is, might take her for a sturdy farmer's wife. But for those who know her as Mélanie, the heroine of my novel *The Bridge of Years,* she is very much more.

SIX

Neighbors Happen

FOR SOME MONTHS after I moved in, I knew the dead better than
the living. I used to climb the hill, up from the open bowl where
the village lies, to the cemetery, to get a sight of the mountains
at sunset, and to take some deep breaths of the larger prospect
from up there. It is a lovely cemetery, lying under a stand of
maples—airy green in spring, gold in autumn—dropping down a
steep incline to a pond one can see in winter. There is something
human and intimate about the atmosphere up there which
comes, I sense, from the fact that it was once inhabited by the
living, was the original site of the village.

I loved the old eighteenth-century gravestones, moon-faced
angels of death carved into the soft slate, and their grim "Me-
mento Moris," but what interested me most was to decipher the

Photograph by Eric Sanford

names. I studied them—Upton, Tolman, Lightfoot, Hardy, French—and in that way I came to know my neighbors before I "knew" them. Sometimes I sat down on the granite bench before the enormous stone memorial in honor of the men who fought in the Revolution, and marveled that such a small place could muster so many to ride down through the leafy roads bringing their muskets to the defense of Lexington. But of course Nelson was very much larger then, a kind of mother village which has seen its children go off on their own to become Munsonville and Harrisville and Chesham. The European in me was amazed by how recent all this history is—just a couple of hundred years!

On those chill autumn evenings the dark came suddenly. When I walked down the hill again, lights would have come on in the few inhabited houses around the green. I passed one on my way home, and wondered what life was like inside it. It looked a little bit like the house of the old woman who lived in a shoe: it needed paint; the roof sagged; a shed at one end seemed about to tumble—and, true, two children came out every morning, to take the school bus. On a day of pouring rain before I had moved in, I had knocked on that door to ask for something. I had almost to force my way in from the downpour to speak to a cross old man who was glaring at me. The roof leaked; a pail stood on the long trestle table covered with unwashed dishes; there was a pile of lumber in one corner, and one wall was unfinished. A violin lay on one chair and a pile of laundry on another. On another occasion I had driven up from Cambridge with Judy late one evening, shortly after I signed the deed, to look at my house. We sat in the car, not wanting to disturb the tenants. Suddenly, out of the dark, there materialized a slender woman in blue jeans who asked us rather sharply what we were doing there. She did not speak like a country woman, and she had an air of authority. I stammered something about having just bought the place, and, slightly chilled, we watched her walk back across the green toward the same house where I had had short shrift from the "cross old man."

So on those autumn evenings I passed by their lighted windows toward my dark ones, feeling a little like a ghost. I soon learned to turn on lights before wandering out at dusk, so, welcomed home by a blaze of light, I could play the childish game of standing outside and peering in at the white walls, the books and flowers, and asking myself, "I wonder who lives here?"

Not until Thanksgiving did any villager except Mr. Upton appear by name. Judy and I and Union Suit had celebrated with a great feast and were sitting by the fire drinking coffee, and Union Suit was still washing his face, when we heard the tinkle of the ancient doorbell. An elderly lady stood at the door, smiling, and repeating a curious phrase that sounded like "Hosh geldiniz." I invited her in, and when she was settled in a chair by the fire, she explained that she was Bessie Lyman from the parsonage, and that she had welcomed us in Turkish. In Turkish? Yes, she and her husband had been missionaries in Turkey for many years; now retired, and a widow, she lived with her sister Myra just back of the church. I noticed that, as she talked, she kept glancing up at the Arabic inscription over my head. Finally she got up to come and look at it more closely.

"Oh yes," she said, "the opening of the Koran!" and proceeded to read it off in Arabic.

How delighted my father would have been at the idea that I had landed in a village where Arabic was spoken! I felt quite provincial suddenly, and was aware for the first time, but not for the last, that Nelson is no ordinary village.

Bessie Lyman had come that day to invite us to tea to meet her sister, and a few days later we found ourselves in their delightful atmosphere among the African violets and the yellow cats in a house filled with mementos of two active lives. For Myra had not stayed home either; she had spent her youth as librarian for a Negro school in Georgia. And now, in her retirement, she gives us her skill to help in the tiny Memorial Library on the green, opening its doors once a week to the children. They come here to meet Peter Rabbit, Charlotte of *Charlotte's Web*, and Stuart Little, Toad of Toad Hall, Winnie the Pooh, and Jo and Black Beauty for the first time.

Tea at the parsonage is tea in the English style; we sit comfortably round a table. Best cups and saucers have been brought out; the silver shines; there are not only hot muffins but ice cream and cake as well. The talk is of everything going on in the world, and sometimes "the world" turns out to be the village.

No doubt it was Bessie and Myra who first introduced me to Miss Morrison. I had become aware that one of the white houses, the only one with a huge barn attached to it, was inhabited by an old lady with a piercing blue glance. This, I now learned, was "Maurie," as everyone calls her. She is a magic person, a kind of Mary Poppins for disturbed children. She has, over the years, restored to normal life one child after another given up for lost by formal schools, and, in some cases, even by mental institutions. For Maurie does not know the meaning of the word "despair" where a human being is concerned. Little by little she has "brought up" her children, done it by infinite patience, hope, and love, done it not by indulgence but by imaginative discipline, done it by being a little like a Nannie, a Nannie of genius. When I moved in Maurie was engaged in her last heroic battle to help a very troubled boy, and I did not really get to know her until several years later. But I caught the burr the first time I heard her speak, for she is a Scot—born in Lewis, the outermost island of the Hebrides.

Sometime after Thanksgiving the Quigleys and I connected at last—he "the cross old man" and she "the distinguished woman" whom I had already met without knowing who they were. I invited them over for a drink.

There were chrysanthemums in the blue jug; the fire was lit in the big fireplace. I was apprehensive that afternoon, as if we were about to take an examination, I and the house together. But I need not have worried. These two people, who had seemed a little alarming before, greeted me warmly; the atmosphere was friendly and easy, and soon Mildred and I were so deep in conversation that I had forgotten we were not old friends. Quig meanwhile was very silent.

He looked at first glance like a countryman. His plaid shirt and heavy boots, a crest of white hair and thick, dark eyebrows over a rugged face—these suggested an outdoor huntin', fishin' man. Only when one came to know him did the extreme sensitivity of the man show through. The eyebrows, for instance, were mobile—did they actually tremble sometimes like the furry antennae of a moth?

I didn't catch all that then; I was too busy listening to the small distinguished person in the wing chair, for she was telling me what I most longed to know, telling me about my immediate predecessor in the house, Cora Tolman, "Aunt Cora." I was learning something about that indomitable, tragic, hunchbacked figure—that she loved flowers passionately; that she did not have an easy time with her second husband; that she was an original who looked at things for herself and spoke in startling and often humorous images; and that Mildred had nursed her through the last illness. And while Mildred talked I learned something about her as well as about "Aunt Cora."

Suddenly Quig, who had been absent though he sat there with his drink in his hand, came back to us.

"Excuse me," he said, "but I have been looking. I am so moved by this furniture . . . it is so beautiful."

It was my first awareness of what I called Quig's "fits of looking." He could be as absorbed in what his eyes registered at such times as a person is whose ears are absorbed in listening to music. Once more the past was weaving itself inextricably into the present. It was wonderful to be able to tell the Quigleys a little about the Flemish furniture, about Wondelgem, and about my parents. And as I did so, I imagined the old *bahut* became animated and glowed softly in the firelight. Things when they are old and beautiful have a life of their own, but it comes to the surface only when someone "sees" them again, as Quig had done. Soon he was telling me something of his past, which explained why he had felt the furniture and its aura so deeply. Later I learned his whole story—a story that proved to me once more that Nelson has gathered into its quiet heart an amazing variety of people and ways of life.

Albert Quigley, to give him his full name for once, was not a native. He came from Maine and had the sea in his blood; his father was a stonecutter; stonecutting had been Quig's first trade. But it surely must have been clear from the start that this boy had in him aspirations, hungers, talents, that would inevitably lead him out of that small company-owned and company-dominated village. He was musical, and taught himself to play the violin and to mend old violins under the tutelage of a violin-maker in the neighborhood, so that he knew his instrument both as craftsman and as musician.

World War I was the crucial experience of his life. He went to France with the Signal Corps, and he came back a changed man. For he came back a painter. He never talked about "war experiences"—what he talked about was France. Quig remembered every village, every line of plane trees along a country road, every plastered stone wall with a geranium on top of it, as if he had seen them yesterday. This unlikely doughboy did not frequent cafés when he had time off; he walked the countryside, going as far as his legs would take him, absorbing France through his very skin. And when the war was over, he stayed on to study at the A.E.F. school outside Barbizon for a year, under what would later come to be known as the "G.I. Bill."

He had undoubted talent, but it was out of the question to earn a living as a landscape or portrait painter, and Quig decided to try photography. He set up shop in Keene. There he met Mildred, and there his real life began. Quig never had an easy time of it, but in his life he was given two great pieces of luck. The first was when he happened on that haunting, intense, reserved face of a young woman whose own circumstances had made her, if not morose, determined to go it alone. She had paid no attention to him when he and two friends of his were seated at her table in the crowded restaurant, nor did she even smile when he inadvertently spilled a glass of water. But he did pay attention to her. And when he saw her walking down the street a few days later, a hat pulled down over her eyes against the world, Quig flipped the hat up and said, "Lets go for a walk!"

That first walk turned out to be a long one, for they went up and down every street that leads off The Square.

If ever a man needed a wife with the courage of a mountain lion, it was Quig, and he found it in Mildred, small and frail-looking but so wiry and nervy that a hurricane could not budge her if she decided to stay put.

These were the two extraordinary people who had come to sit by my fire that memorable November afternoon. We plunged right into friendship. If I had, before then, sometimes felt a stab of loneliness as dark settled in, I was not to be lonely in Nelson again. I had once more in my life stumbled into "family."

At that time Mildred went out every morning to nurse Mr. Upton's wife and to take care of his house. She has not, since I have known her, had time off from hard work, yet she always has time to sit down, smoke a cigarette, and talk about the things that really matter, from a sick kitten to the state of the world. How many times I have crossed the green with a heavy heart, only to come home an hour later nourished in those deep recesses where life, however hard, is somehow always in touch with a source that has renewal in it.

I soon found out that I could talk to Quig about my work as one can talk only with a fellow craftsman. Our crafts were different, but we had the same difficulty in getting started, the same despair sometimes at the end of the morning's struggle when nothing had quite "come out," the same hours of sudden triumph when it did. Often one or the other of us would cross the green at noon to exchange news on the state of the work. Quig's life had been a perpetual war with material circumstances to find time to paint at all, yet I never heard him complain about that. He blamed himself for not doing better, and in his sixties —when I first knew him—attacked each new day with the anxious eagerness of a boy. There were a good many things besides painting always on his mind—making frames, practicing the violin, playing for country dances, and, when things got really tight, working on the night shift at the Harrisville woolen mill. Making ends meet meant doing a hundred and one odd jobs.

But fortunately he had a haven when the mood to paint was on him—the second floor of the abandoned schoolhouse. There he had installed a little wood stove; there he had a great empty space and good light; there he could take refuge from all the unfinished business at home and spend hours in front of a canvas. And there I used to find him at the end of the morning. I don't suppose we ever talked about painting without Alec James's name coming up. I sensed how terrible a gap this "friend of the work" had left when he died, how Quig missed Alec's touch, Alec's warmth, Alec's fits of gaiety, and how he longed for Alec's eye to criticize or approve a morning's work. For his encounter with Alec James had been the second great piece of luck in Quig's life, as his encounter with Mildred had been the first.

They were an extraordinary pair, Alexander James, son of the philosopher William James, born into the New England aristocracy, and Albert Quigley, stonecutter's son, millworker, fiddler; but their differences fused in the passion they shared for their art and craft. For Alec, Quig must have been like an older brother, less volatile, sturdier, less of a race horse, able to share in the wild fits of humor that released the tension in the younger man. To Quig, Alec brought the standards and know-how of the highly professional craftsman and critic. He taught Quig a great deal about techniques, brushes, canvas, taught him expensive tastes in these matters, and helped him to pay for them by employing Quig as his own framemaker and by getting him commissions from other painters. Above all, Alec took Quig's painting seriously and held him to it, for art must be nourished by faith, the faith of an equal. For Alec, "dear old Quig," as he called him, represented, no doubt, the pure, unadulterated person, free of the pressure of the professional artist under which Alec lived. Like any real friendship—and this was a great one—it sprang out of mutual need and was nourished from mutual riches. No one outside the two men will ever know the depth of it.

But without Mildred, who stayed home with the three little children, none of it would have been possible. It was her generosity and understanding that left Quig free to come and go into that other world of Dublin. Even very good marriages have their times of strain and stress. It is the measure of the reality of this one that the intense "engagement" between Alec and Quig was allowed free play, without a shadow.

And what fun Quig and Mildred had together! That was what I felt whenever I stopped in to find them playing cribbage or putting gold leaf on a frame, or just sitting and talking, a cat on the arm of Mildred's big chair and Honey, the asthmatic spaniel, lying at Quig's feet.

Quig was more complex than he seemed. Although he lived in a perpetual, if lively, disorder in his own house, he loved ceremony. He was not a great drinker, but, as he often told me, what he loved was the ceremony around a drink, the fire lit, the flowers on the table, the enclosed, peaceful hour at the end of the day, the good talk. We never met, we three, without feeling that something of moment had happened between us; we never talked without the talk turning on "real things"—relationship and all its mysteries, art and all its mysteries, the natural world and all its mysteries. For me, to be with the Quigleys was to come home to the values with which I had grown up, values that often seem anachronistic in the United States today. For one thing, the world we shared, in ceremony, was completely uncompetetive. Status—social or professional—had no place in it. We conversed like three Chinese philosophers about the things that *really* matter, and sometimes we had a good laugh about those that don't.

When I had a poem hot off the griddle, I read it to them. Poetry, like chamber music, thrives best on a few listeners, but those one or two are essential. The poem does not live until it has been *heard*. What would have become of me that long winter if there had been no one to listen? Always I felt that whatever I had managed to say was being considered with the utmost attention. Always I felt that the intention, at least, had fallen on fertile ground. The response was in character. Mildred, always articulate, often carried the poem a step farther, gave it a surprising, original insight of her own which might send me back to make a revision. Quig reacted with that feeling silence which is the accolade every poet longs to receive. He was easily moved but never superficially moved, and utterance came hard to him at such moments. I must add to the life-giving silences of Nelson Quig's way of listening to a poem.

SEVEN

The Edge of Nowhere

WINTER IS THE SEASON when both animals and humans get stripped down to the marrow, but many animals hibernate, take the winter easy as it were; we humans are exposed naked to the currents of elation and depression. Here at Nelson it is the time of the most extraordinary light and the most perfect silence. When the first snow floats down on the rock-hard earth, first a flake at a time, then finally in soft white curtains, an entirely new silence falls. It feels as if one were being wound up into a cocoon, sealed in. There will be no escape, the primitive person senses, always with the same shiver of apprehension. At the same time, there is elation. One is lifted up in a cloud, a little above the earth, for soon there is no earth to be seen, only whiteness—whiteness without a shadow, while the snow falls. Is

Photograph by Eleanor Blair

it dawn or dusk? Who can tell? And this goes on all night and occasionally all the next day, until there is no way out of the house. I am sealed in tight. Many times during the night I wake to listen, listen, but there is no sound at all. The silence is as thick and soft as wool. Will the snow ever stop falling?

But when at last the sun comes out again, we are born into a pristine world, into the snow light. The house has become a ship riding long white slopes of waves. The light! It is like living in a diamond in this house where the white walls reflect the snow outside. There are shadows again, but now they are the most brilliant blue, lavender, even purple at dusk. And sooner or later I must push hard to open the front door against the drifts and get myself out with seed for the bird feeders. Then, when I come back to sit at my desk, I look out on an air full of wings as they come to dart, swoop, and settle—jays, nuthatches, chicka-dees, evening grosbeaks, woodpeckers, making a flurry of bril-liant color across the white. The plows go roaring down the road, and I am safe inside with a fire burning in the study, lifted up on such excitement at my changed world that I can hardly sit still.

These are the irresistible moods that the world outside brings on, the good storms that literally change the air and change our minds at the same time. In that first winter, the weather itself was the great adventure, for I did not know how it would be, whether I could get out, for instance! But I soon learned that here, deep in the country, we are far better taken care of than city people when there is a blizzard. I have never had to wait more than a few hours before the plow comes charging into my drive to clear a path for the car—also to leave great piles of snow against the doors of house and barn and so provide winter exercise for the housebound.

That first winter was not all joy and discovery. I was to learn about anxiety, isolation, the dark side of the moon of solitude. Even a new life does not exorcise old demons, and my demons will, perhaps, never be exorcised entirely. But I had made the decision to move into the country out of powerful need, the need to try at least to come to terms with them. I was deliberately cutting life back to the marrow, and this meant that I had cut myself off from all that helps us balance acute depression against the gentle demands of day-to-day living—from family life, in my case the dear rites and traditions of my life with Judy, getting a meal together, going for a walk, playing with the cat in the evening, from all that clothes the naked soul and comforts it.

I suppose that the worst of my demons has always been impatience, a fierce and wilful driver inside me who says, "Make haste, make haste!" And at first my new life, far from quelling this demon, seemed to have given him even greater authority. Especially in winter, when I am more or less alone with my work, the pressure increases as the doubts flow in. The crisis of middle age has to do as much as anything with a catastrophic anxiety about time itself. How has one managed to come to the meridian and still be so far from the real achievement one had dreamed possible at twenty? And I mean achievement as a human being as well as within a career.

But against the demons, against my own lacks and conflicts, against all that felt unfinished, stood the house.

> "The house stayed by me, full of light, yet solid.
> However many ashes had to be raked out,
> However many childish hopes were shed,
> I learned from grief and learned to make my bed.
> This was a life claim I was staking out."

There are no quick rewards for the depressed person. It is a matter of making a channel and then guiding one's boat through it, day by day. For me the channel has always been work, the writing of poems and novels, and each of these has been a way of coming to understand what was really happening to me. Experience is the fuel; I would live my life burning it up as I go along, so that at the end nothing is left unused, so that every piece of it has been consumed in the work.

One does not ever give up if one is a writing animal, and if one has, over the years, created the channel of a routine. Those hours of total concentration on something that comes from deep in the self, yet must be looked at and handled objectively as it goes down on paper, are bound to be fruitful. I am happy while I am writing. The demons come as soon as I stop and consider what I have done, as the critic takes over from the creator. Colette asks somewhere, "What have I to teach, unless it be self-doubt, to those who since early youth have become secretly infatuated by self-love rather than by self-torture?"

The demons of self-doubt may torture, but it is to a good, a necessary end. They are the demons who kept Colette revising a few sentences for a whole morning, and I hope they will never leave me in peace! The bad demons have to do with what happens to a piece of work after it is finished; they come to plague with their deadly questions when the reviews appear. And they are very much harder to subdue because they have to be endured in silence. And because, unlike every other kind of experience, the experience they bring cannot be used, cannot be burned up or transformed into a work of art.

These demons, which might be called the demons of reputation, have two masks, and I do not know which is more distressing. There is the demon who wears the mask of rage: Why have I not been recognized? A young writer may be able to turn that demon away by taking refuge in the delusion of his genius, by thinking as a child does, "They'll be sorry when I am dead!" For the middle-aged professional writer there is no such consolation. He has, willy-nilly, become a realist. He has to face the other demon who wears the mask of self-doubt: Why have I failed? Where have I been self-indulgent, lazy, not honest enough? Or is my failure written into my very bones?

This demon sometimes comes to tell me that, because I was born in Europe and have no definite American social background to work from, I am disabled as novelist from the start. Sometimes what he has to tell me is that I have been fatally divided in loyalty between two crafts, that of the novel and that of poetry.

But whether I contend with rage or with self-doubt they both spring from the same source, the fact that, although I am lucky enough to have been published from the start, I have never experienced real success, either that success which is given, and can only be given, by serious critical attention, or the other success which comes from reaching the big public. As a writer I have had to exist in a kind of Purgatory . . . perhaps a salutary one. I have seen too many instances of what seems to be Heaven not to know in my saner moments that I have been lucky in my Purgatory. What happens if a first book achieves instant recognition on the grand scale? Only an increase in the weight of indecision that plagues us all about "what next?" Only a huge burden *already* of a past that has to be met on its own terms, which means a book as good the next time. Success means an invasion from the world, not only of letters but of requests for attention of all sorts that consume energy and are all, whether gratifying or not, hazards, interruptions for the central person, the writer who must pull out of himself another work. How often a "successful" book must have become for its creator the enemy, an enemy he can never entirely destroy and be done with, but which will haunt his nights and days! I know of one case where this tension built up to suicide.

But though, in my Purgatory, I have escaped the hazards of "success," I have had to try to master rage. One cannot fight for one's work. That is the great paradox. Even if an atrociously unfair review appears, one cannot answer; one must simply contain the poison, and it *is* poison when twenty years' work may be brushed aside with a sneer because it has accidentally fallen into the hands of a critic with an ax to grind. That happened to me when the *Selected Poems* came out. And in that case it took months to recover from the poison.

On the other hand, if sometimes unlucky in the critics, I have been lucky in slowly getting my books through, across them, like secret agents, into the territory of the readers. There I know that I am welcome. The welcome is not measured in sales—now always respectable but never enormous—but in little things that have come to my attention, such as the fact that in the Detroit

Public Library my books have to be rebound every six months. Sometimes I am discovered by a reader who writes to commend a work written twenty years ago. Purgatory is made bearable by these innumerable personal messages—messages from the unknown reader who answers a book as if it were a letter. How wonderful it was when the poet H. D., whom I had loved since I was a child, wrote me after my first novel came out, as did the poet Haniel Long from Santa Fe, a letter which began a long friendship. The admiration of a fellow writer brings a flush to the cheek, like getting an A in school, but for me it is even more heartening to be told that a farmer's wife has pinned a poem up over her sink. The rage comes in when reviewers and critics put up a wall between the writer and such a woman. How is one to get through the wall? Only by going quietly on one's way sending out the secret agents.

There are quicker means, no doubt, of getting through, and one of them is to make it one's business to cultivate the right people. Like any highly competitive world, the world of literature is controlled at any given time by a comparatively small number of "names," without whose approval no prize is given and no important review appears. I have seen a good many reputations come and go in the thirty years since I began to publish. I have a built-in revulsion against this seeking out of the powers. Perhaps it is that I really don't enjoy seeing writers very much. On the whole I prefer not to talk "shop"; I find myself nourished by a craftsman from another field—a painter, a carpenter, a musician, a vinegrower, but disturbed beyond what is normal, perhaps, by contact with other writers.

My father was as inept about relations in his academic world, and for the same reason. I suppose the reason is a combination of pride, perhaps even vanity, and innocence. But he knew, and taught me by his example, that pride and innocence are the *sine qua non* of distinguished work, and I might add, of peace of mind: "I knew a phoenix in my youth so let them have their day."

I believe that eventually my work will be seen as a whole, all the poems and all the novels, as the expression of a vision of life which, though unfashionable all the way, has validity, as did my father's whole work for the same reason.

But what if this hope proves to be an illusion? There is still then the very real comfort that it is not ignoble to serve a hard master for little reward, without faltering. Henry James has said it for all of us when he put these words into the mouth of a writer in one of his stories: "A second chance—*that's* the delusion. There never was to be but one. We work in the dark—we do what we can—we give what we have. Our doubt is our passion and our passion is our task. The rest is the madness of art."

In such terms I myself answer the demons. But of course the only real way to keep them off is to shut the world out. One of the gifts this house in Nelson has brought me is that it seems easier to do this here than anywhere else I have ever lived. Is it because we all live on the edge of nowhere in Nelson? It is literally "out of the world." What takes place here when I am working takes place between me and God.

But it is just here that the worst of the demons, the hardest one to handle, makes his appearance. How can I be sure that all the years I have sat at a desk add up to anything worth having, as against what I might have done had I, for instance, devoted myself to teaching underprivileged children? This is the demon of guilt who points out that what Colette calls a life of self-torture may in fact be the purest self-indulgence.

For a single woman the question is acute. She is not buttressed by a family and the responsibilities of a family, nor, on the other hand, by the Rule and the Community which support a religious. She has made a choice that cuts her off from a lot of things most people consider life, for the sake of something else, something both chancy and intangible. No wonder anxiety is the constant attendant of such a one!

My anxiety that first winter went almost beyond control, and part of it was that I suddenly had to face the fact that I do not have an indefinite time ahead. I was beginning a new life in middle age, but I was also carrying on from twenty years or

more devoted to two arts. My stance had always been that I
would go on growing and do better, both as poet and as novelist, *in time*. Now, quite suddenly, time seemed to shrink. The
tide might even be ebbing, for all I knew, before I had tasted it
at the flood.

It became more necessary than ever to eliminate waste. "I
wasted time and now doth time waste me" was no longer a
beautiful phrase but a probing reality. During the snow-bright
days and the long evenings sitting by the fire or pacing the floor,
I began to understand that for me "waste" had not come from
idleness, but perhaps from pushing myself too hard, from not
being idle enough, from listening to the demon who says "make
haste." I had allowed the wrong kind of pressure to build up,
that kind which brings frustration in its wake. I was helped by
Louise Bogan's phrase "Let life do it." But what kind of life?

Just how far and to what end would solitude take me? And
how can one have the courage to shut life out when it knocks at
the door? Already I was beginning to know a few of the people
scattered over the hills around Nelson. Although in some ways
remote, Nelson is only two hours from Boston, and even in winter there is a social life, a sophisticated one. Now and then I was
invited out to dinner. I found these occasions intoxicating, for at
them I not only met a new group of charming people but always
learned something about the country, or about Nelson history,
about hunting or fishing, and I suspect that I was the perfect lis-
tener for many a tall tale. I was at the same time delighted and
uneasy. If I began to accept invitations, I should soon be giving
invitations myself, and the whole atmosphere of the house would
be subtly changed. I was surprised to discover how strongly I
felt about *not* having cocktail parties here, as if the house had
already, in so short a time, begun to change me in wholly unexpected ways. So, as the pressure contained in a social life, however modest, made itself felt, it was an awkward time for me.
How to refuse kindness, the open door, reject so much good will
toward a stranger?

The answer did not come easy that first year, but I finally

came to terms with it, and I have never regretted the decision I made then, when I had my back against the wall in so many ways. But at least it was my wall and I had chosen it, "no shelter but a grave demand." The answer became "no" to any purely social invitation, however tempting. The people I would choose to see I would see, in a casual way that involves pure friendship without the necessity of either accepting or returning formal invitations.

I am aware that I have shut myself out of a great deal of pleasure, but I had not come here for pleasure, and that was that. I might add that one of the miracles of Nelson is that everyone has understood. I used to think, in the years when I spent some time in Vouvray in France, and came to know the vinegrowers around Grace Dudley's house there, that I would never again find a place where I could be so taken for granted as a worker, in just the way a carpenter or a farmer who has a daily job to do is taken for granted. But here at Nelson I have found just that respect for the professional craftsman. It is only city people who turn up and think nothing of interrupting the day's work! No neighbor of mine here calls uninvited.

Through all these anxieties, hazards, losses, depressions and moments of elation, I had a strong and life-enhancing support in the house itself. There was no day that strange, vivid winter not redeemed by some piece of magic. Music, flowers, books, letters from outside, the changing light, the marvelous silences—none except the last two were new to me, but all were now framed in a new way, to be experienced at a new depth, because of my isoation.

In some ways I had lived too rich a life and lived it too fast. What had looked for a while like a full stop was proving to be just the opposite, a chance for renewal, not so much through new life as through having the time and the chance to absorb what I already had in my pouch, so to speak. The poet who had pored with passionate absorption over many a human face was, although she did not yet quite accept the fact, moving into a new phase. Just at dusk the hills that surround the village sometimes take the afterglow. They and the high church steeple are all lit up, making a luminous bowl in which the already shadowy village lies . . . a vision like this was subtly replacing in my attention the changing light on a human face.

The dark came suddenly, flowed into the house, and filled me sometimes with a second of dread. It was time then to light the fire and put on the lights in the big room, like round moons in their Japanese paper lanterns, time to come back to a human world, where a Japanese print or a blue-and-white jug bring a long train of thought with them into the warm room.

If I got snowed in, I could shovel myself out. The trees, which groaned in a heart-rending way in storms, did not fall. Though it did often feel like the edge of nowhere, I found that I was very much alive on the edge of nowhere.

I was nevertheless haunted by something Mildred had said one of the first times she and Quig came over. As she looked around appreciatively at the changes I had made, at the open, spacious place the cramped old house had become, she said a startling thing—"It has not been a happy house." Perhaps she meant that now the house would come into its happiness. But in my state of perilous balance between hope and despair, the words hit me with the force of a fairy godmother's curse. Just as in a fairy tale the princess must ponder how to turn the curse into a blessing, I have pondered these words. I cannot say that I have been exactly happy here . . . too many of the people I love never come here, or come rarely. I have wept bitter tears in this house. At any moment solitude may put on the face of loneliness. Life here has been, from the start, a challenge. And that is the point—not, perhaps, happiness, but life lived at its most aware and intense. Would not "Aunt Cora" have said as much when the first old-fashioned rose by the granite step, that rose so tightly folded into its hairy bud, opened each spring? Not happiness, perhaps, but something like New England itself—struggle, occasional triumph over adversity, above all the power to endure and to be renewed. For here the roses grow beside the granite.

EIGHT

Mud Season

IN MOST PLACES spring begins in March, but in this ornery part
of the country April finds us still bogged down in limbo. When
crocuses are out in Cambridge, we may still have a blizzard. Extreme weather brings a certain exhilaration with it; what is
harder to bear is the long wait in a soggy gray world. The rocks
stand up, raw and desolate in the colorless meadow; the trees
look thin and exhausted, and the longer days only accentuate the
sour wilderness feel of it all, a meager wilderness, all stains and
patches and broken stone walls. I have learned that April is a
good time to go out lecturing, to go toward spring long before it
reaches Nelson, when hepaticas are lifting their delicate blue
and white heads in Indiana, and the Judas tree and white dogwood are in flower in Kentucky. Almost anywhere is better than

Photograph by Eleanor Blair

here in "mud season." But that first year, full of expectation, ex-
hilarated by having survived the winter, I did not know the ordeals to come.

In February I had pored, enchanted, over the seed catalogues and their glossy photographs, dreaming the still nonexist-
ent garden. My idea was to combine vegetables and picking
flowers in a plot just behind the house. Sitting at the kitchen
table in a snowstorm I had joyously imagined Chinese peas
(eaten pod and all), zucchini, cucumber, every kind of lettuce. I
went wild on flowers—cosmos, zinnia, marigolds, elegant salpi-
glossis, annual phlox, delphinium, bachelor's-buttons—with a
total disregard of how all this was to be fitted into one small
patch. After all, one has to be allowed some extravagance in
February. By April all those little packages of hope were stowed
away in a big tin breadbox, in case a mouse decided on nastur-
tium (delicious!) as an aperitif before going on to candle ends,
soap, and any crumbs I might have left lying about.

By April I wandered about outside, peering under the spruce
and hemlock boughs I had strewn over the flower beds to see
whether anything was coming up. Would the peonies, the phlox,
have survived the winter? So far there was no sign.

Then one evening I heard a slight, shrill, continuous singing,
a little like distant sleigh bells. And I suddenly remembered
what Tink had said when we sat on a pile of lumber eating
lunch that summer day—"The peepers! Wait till you hear them
when it seems as if spring would never come!" The long wait
was coming to an end. The brooks, unfrozen at last, rich in
melted snow, ran impetuously over and around boulders, making
pools of brown foam wherever they were impeded, and tiny
waterfalls and whirlpools. And I understood better than before
Gerard Manley Hopkins's fascination with the patterns of moving water as, remembering the exquisite drawings in his Note-
books, I myself bent to observe closely the rich flow of spirals
and swirls, curling themselves around a rock. What a thrill when
the first skunk cabbage came out, thrusting its baroque green
through moldy old leaves! I was starved for color as well as for

motion in the static world, and that first bright green of the skunk cabbage was a tonic. But the greatest change was going on in the air overhead: skies were a gentler blue; soft white clouds piled up into quick rainfall, and the sunsets lost their winter brilliance as bright gold changed to pale gold, crimson to pink, against a hyacinthine sky. Best of all, one could smell earth again, after the long frozen months when only woodsmoke sweetened the icy air. A pair of phoebes appeared, flicking their tails on the telephone wires; they were building a nest under the porch eaves, as they have every year since. A bunch of snowdrops pushed up through the sodden grass by the front step.

It was the beginning all right, but there was still a long way to go. This brief explosion was followed by weeks when nothing happened. It rained. I learned what mud season means when the car got stuck again and again, making deep ruts in the driveway. The grass was still gray. Since I could not reach the dump on wheels, I had to haul the ash cans inch by inch up a steep incline slithery with mud. It snowed again. It froze again. (At least once each spring, I see the daffodils and crocuses completely covered by snow after they have flowered.) I was to learn that the snow is kind—"poor man's fertilizer," they call it —but that frost is the killer. And we have had frost in Nelson at one time or another in every month except July. So through all of April and through most of May we are still suspended.

The birds come before the leaves and flowers—warblers on their way north, the first fat robins to stay, running and stopping, running and stopping, to pull a worm with their knowing beaks. Swallows come back, to fly restlessly in and out of the broken windowpane I have left as a swallow door in the barn. And one morning that first spring I looked out of the window and caught sight of a bluebird sitting on a granite post just a few feet away!

I do not really mind the long wait, but I do mind the fact that when spring finally comes, it comes with such a rush that one cannot keep track of all that is happening. This swift change from not enough to too much is disturbing. Where to look?

What to do? Where to begin? Who can keep up with a spring that comes and goes, it would seem, in the space of a clap of thunder? that takes you by the throat, as it were? The maples, which had looked so old and forlorn all winter, were suddenly covered with small green umbrella-flowers. Shall I ever manage to be present in the hour they open? Always they have just arrived while my back was turned.

At last, when I tossed the hemlock branches onto a big pile for burning, I saw that everything I had planted was alive. The phlox was already there in green fleshed-out humps. Tulips and daffodils had pierced through, and the small red spears of the peonies were above ground. I went out on a warm day to measure off the picking garden to prepare for seed-planting, stopping to look at the apple tree by the barn, covered with bright pink buds, each branch as rich and stiff as coral. The sun was deliciously warm on my back; I worked so hard that I did not realize what was happening. It was only when I went in that I discovered large swollen red bites all over my neck, wrists, and ankles. Black flies!

The truth is that every season in the country has its special ordeals, but what made the first year both exhilarating and difficult was that I came on them unprepared. I had heard of black flies, of course, and that a seasoned tourist keeps away from New Hampshire in May and June, when they are at their worst. Now I understood why.

Whenever I went out, at whatever time of day, a black cloud hovered over my head, a cloud of flies that settled, one by one, in every exposed place, crept under my glasses to bite my eyelids, crept into my ears, under the cuffs of my shirt, and up the legs of my jeans. Years later I discovered a remedy only a little less disgusting than the bites. It is thick, brown, and smells of tar, and if I cover my face, neck, hands, and legs with this "Woodsman's Dope," I can work more or less in peace. But brief snatches of work out of doors, when the spirit moves, are out of the question, since I have to undress and have a bath after each expedition.

The black flies could be endured—I had not reckoned with the woodchucks! Visually speaking, a woodchuck, especially a baby woodchuck, is an endearing animal; round as a teddy bear, it sits up and hugs itself like a squirrel. My first emotion when I saw a mother with two babies playing in front of the barn was joyful surprise. The babies rolled over on their backs; the mother nibbled grass; it all seemed like a spring scherzo. But when I looked out the kitchen window the next morning and saw that all the new phlox had been eaten back to the root, the dear little creatures became deadly enemies.

Until then I thought I had learned that if I didn't panic I could handle any crisis that came up. This was different. I dashed out a hundred times a day, waving my arms and shouting, knowing perfectly well that the marauders would return as soon as my back was turned—and of course the stone wall was a perfect apartment house with many safe entrances and exits for them. I lay awake at night, wondering whether they were out or in. I was up at dawn.

But the phlox grew back, and by then there was a lot of green stuff in the woods; surely the animals would find something as good to eat elsewhere. I could not accept that my garden might be destroyed without ever having existed! That seemed to me preposterous, unfair, not to be borne.

Then the day came when I looked out and saw that the phlox had been eaten down a second time! I burst into tears of woe and frustration, and on an impulse called the Newt Tolmans. Janet recognized a note of desperation and assured me that Newt would be over with his gun within the hour.

I don't suppose I have ever seen a more welcome arrival than Newt in his jeep. He came up the porch steps with a gun in his hand and a twinkle in his eye.

"Here I am," he said. "What's up?"

I explained my ridiculous plight, of trying to make a garden against what appeared to be insuperable odds, and—God bless him!—he didn't laugh. He said quite vehemently, "Why didn't you call for help, woman? That's what neighbors are for!"

We spent an hour drinking martinis and talking while we stood at the kitchen counter and watched and waited. Sure enough, a family of woodchucks appeared again, and Newt crept to the door like an Indian and got in a couple of shots, just too late to catch the wary and speedy creatures. How could I ever have dreamed that I would *want* an animal killed? But, after all, the phlox too was a live thing and had proved its resilience; the woodchuck had plenty to eat in the woods. Must they have caviar? Newt did kill one before he left, for Newt is a very good shot.

This visit did not dispose of the problem but it gave me new courage; in time of need help would be forthcoming. And from more than one direction. A few mornings later I heard secretive footsteps go by my bedroom window, and looked out, startled, to see Ted Murdough out in the field with his gun. He came by every morning for a week on his way to work, and after that the woodchuck got the message . . . or perhaps they found something in the woods that they liked better than delicate perennials.

The indomitable phlox came up a third time, and even flowered later on in the summer. So I have learned, through the years, to be more philosophical. I have also invested in a rifle. It has to be reloaded after every shot, so it is not a very effective weapon, but it makes a loud bang, and that is a comfort. It is more dignified to go out with a rifle than to rush out waving one's arms and screaming. I do not shoot to kill or wound but to scare, and repeated scaring does have an effect, so that rifle has added a good deal to my composure and self-reliance.

Self-reliance? Yes, but that first spring I had to learn dependency too. By crying for help and seeing help come from several directions, I began to learn what the village is all about: on the one hand, respect for privacy, and on the other, awareness of each other's needs. So, however solitary some of us may look to an outsider, we are in truth part of an invisible web and supported by its presence.

Help does materialize in a most astonishing way, as if some

signal flashed off into space at a moment of need. Once one of
my cats had been chased to the very top of a thin, tall locust. I
had called myself hoarse, had pleaded in vain, had gone in to let
her think things over, had come back hopefully only to be met
by terrified mews but not the slightest attempt to come down.
Just then a car stopped on the road. When a stranger got out
and walked across the lawn toward me, I supposed that he
wanted to ask directions. But he had seen what was happening
and had taken the trouble to stop in order to offer his help.

"The darned cat won't come down," I said crossly. For what
could *he* do about it?

"I used to be a fireman," he said, stripped off his coat, shin-
nied up thirty feet or more, caught the cat, and brought her
down in a trice.

I stammered my thanks, still too much of a city person not to
be wholly amazed by such unexpected kindness.

I can count on help in moments of real desperation, but for
three years I had to rely on casual encounters or lucky chance to
find a man to do this job or that which I could not manage
alone. Most of the men around the village work on the roads,
grading and cutting brush in summer, plowing in winter. They
have their hands full just keeping us rolling. But I had not come
to the country only to prove to myself that I could master various problems to do with cutting grass or pruning trees or making
a garden where none had been before. I had come to write.
There were times when I felt overwhelmed by these practical
matters. But I always came back to the reality—that the problems or ordeals connected with life in the country are enriching
in some way even when they seem like interruptions and bring
frustration rather than fruition in their wake. Problems to do
with climate, with snow or drought or high wind, problems to do
with growing things, bring one right down to the marrow. They
quickly become metaphor in the mind; they are the stuff of poetry. And there is never loss, the deadly dull loss that life in the
city almost always means. The loss of time spent battling one's
way home in an airless subway cannot be compared, for exam-

ple, with the loss of time spent in getting a cat down out of a tree! And chasing a woodchuck is, on the whole, more fun than chasing a taxi.

But there were times that first spring—and have been since —when I asked myself whether I had undertaken more than I could manage. A place like this is more like a novel than a poem—complex, never quite "finished," operated on extended time, a balancing of many themes against each other. Work on it cannot be finished in one quick push. It must be resumed spring after spring, when black flies and woodchucks come back. It cannot be neglected for long—or you find yourself back where you started. A place like this must be fashioned and re-fashioned inch by inch. You wait and see. You wait and hope. You wait and work.

What I needed, of course, was someone who would stay at my side, who would bring with him many kinds of lore that I do not possess, who would not panic as I sometimes do, a steady worker through all the seasons.

NINE

Perley Cole

OUT OF THE MAGIC that is Nelson, the person I needed was on
the way, as the Quigleys had been on the way that first autumn
although we did not meet for months. Perley Cole did not come
into my life for three years.

At first—it seems incredible now—we were hardly aware of
his presence in the village. We saw lights in the old house up the
hill back of the brick schoolhouse, and figured the deer would no
longer come down of an autumn night to pick windfalls from the
orchard there. Someone had moved in, and that is usually good
news. We didn't know who he was, nor why he had come. It
takes time to penetrate the thickets of private life in Nelson, and
I suppose it must have been several months before I ran into
Perley Cole, at the dump, for at that time I was still hauling my

Photograph by Eleanor Blair

own rubbish, unaware that it might be possible to get someone
to do it for me. We introduced ourselves formally among the ash
cans, and I remember admiring the neat way he had painted his
old pick-up, black with a red lining. It looked shipshape in a
way that few cars around here do, and he himself had an air
about him—an old man, but an old man with a keen eye and a
look of being able to command the situation whatever it might
be.

Then one June day, the ancient bell on my front door tinkled
rather more imperatively than usual, and there he was. He
launched at once into a long speech which managed to seem
laconic because of the manner in which it was delivered. It went
something like this: "I know I'm an old man, an old fool some
might say, but I've done some farming here and there in my
time, and it might happen that you could need some help . . .
Mind you, I ain't goin' to starve, one way or t'other, and I have
plenty to do on my own place, but . . ."

I let him know that there were about a million things that
needed doing, and pointed out a few of them.

"I'll be around one of these days," he said, and vanished.

It was my first experience of his abrupt departures. Every
now and then Perley comes to a boil, and utters. When he has
uttered, he vanishes into thin air. It can be disconcerting until
you get used to it. He is shy and touchy, and I have come to believe that he vanishes because he is suddenly afraid that the answer he has elicited may not be the one he wants to hear.

I watched him walk away that day, his back slightly stooped,
his stride the long slow stride of the farmer who can keep going
from daylight to dark without tiring. And I thought over the
face I had just seen for the second time, an American Gothic
face, lean, sharply lined, with a high forehead and a long stubborn chin, a sharply defined nose, shy, piercing eyes. Why had
he settled here among us? "I'm an old man," he had said, but
there was a certain fierceness in the tone that clearly meant "an
untamed old man."

During the interval between our meeting at the dump and

his call, a good deal had happened on his place. It had been spruced up like nothing we had seen around here lately. Not only had the house itself been painted and the barn rebuilt and reroofed, but the meadow around it had been scythed down. Beds of flowers had made their appearance around the granite rocks. The apple trees had been pruned. The untamed old man was clearly a man of many skills, and he had standards we were not used to seeing. It is wonderful, in a village like this, to see a derelict place reclaimed. It somehow gives us all a lift as we struggle to keep the wilderness from taking over.

Had he been serious, I wondered? Had I put him off by saying the wrong thing? By being too eager, or not eager enough? For I sensed already that this was a man of prickly pride, sensitivity, touchiness, shyness.

Then early one morning, I was woken by a soft sound I could not place, a kind of whispering out in the field between house and barn. From my bed, I pulled the shade up and looked out on a clear bright summer morning, the dew shining on the grass, and there was Perley Cole scything down the jungle. It was the first time I had seen a man scything (even around here we are motorized these days). I watched the long steady sweeps, and how often he stopped and stood the scythe up to whet it— watched and hugely enjoyed the whole operation, repeated over and over, as if in slow motion, the continuous rhythm of it, and the man himself, as tall and angular as his tool. I saw how he handled it with a wary, loving touch. And I saw, too, that this was no rough-and-ready job but a matter of skill and grace. When I went out, later on, he was on his knees trimming with a sickle, although the scythe itself had been used so delicately that only a perfectionist would have seen the need for additional work around the edges. The old barn stood up now as trim as could be.

"See that?" Perley said, lifting the scythe to show me. "Made in England. I wouldn't take a hundred dollars for it!"

The collar of his dark-gray shirt was turned in, and I could see a dew of sweat on his throat; his eyes looked dark blue in the morning light, and his cheeks were pink. There, triumphant, he was surely in the prime of life, and I would never have guessed that he was then over seventy. But he has learned to handle himself as skillfully as a fine tool.

We didn't talk much that day, nor for many days to come. But gradually he shaped and pruned and cleared the place for me. And as he worked I saw that I had lived here for three years in ignorance. Now the light was beginning to dawn. One of the first revelations was what a little pruning can do. Perley trimmed out three small trees around a rock that stands in the middle of my big meadow and suddenly the whole large scene had a focus. You could rest your eyes somewhere. Little by little he enlarged the "lawn" to include all the rough field between house and barn, and brought back the front green to something delightful to behold. He would have none of my power motor. "I wouldn't be seen dead with one of those G— d— noisy bastards," he informed me in that half-aggressive, half-apologetic tone of voice I have come to know so well. He assured me that he could do a better job with my hand machine. Could he? I wondered, for the area is large. After the first time around I was convinced, and I finally gave the power motor away. You don't offer Paderewski a player piano!

Little by little we began to tame each other, finding our way slowly into friendship, sealed with many a glass of sherry when Perley knocked off at noon. The sherry is downed in one gulp. Down it goes, and then, after a moment, up comes a story.

"Court's in session. Now you listen to me!"

I sit on the kitchen stool, drink my sherry slowly, and listen.

So it is that I have come to know a good deal about him, about him and his "bird," as he sometimes calls Angie, and about Parker, their son, who came back from World War II with a permanent cloak of silence around him, as shy as a deer. Parker and his mother are made of the same delicate stuff, but Perley arrived in this world weighing eleven pounds and screaming. He was the youngest of four brothers, and he was not the favorite; he ran away at twelve to work for a neighboring farmer. "I was

not one to hang on my mother's tit!" he told me with savage
pride. By the time he was eighteen he was a man and he knew
whom he was going to marry. "But first the cage, then the bird,"
he told me, and he did not propose to Angie until he could offer
her a house and ten acres of land, which he had bought for $620
from two old-lady schoolteachers who were retiring. He got it
because they wanted him to have it. "And I didn't pay a cent
down," he told me to prove how good his credit was in that
neighborhood.

The young couple had barely settled in when a friend turned
up from the county jail and said, "I need you, Perley."

Perley Cole was the youngest guard they had ever had, but
he had eyes in the back of his head, and I can imagine that he
was both fierce and just. He has told me that he could size up
the troublemakers the day they arrived, and it was for that
prescience, no doubt, that he was respected. At any rate con-
demned men asked that it be young Perley to lead them to the
gallows. His myth-making nature thrived in the prison. I have
come to understand that he lives in a heroic world of his own
making, where everything is a little larger than life-size, where
he expects the worst and is ready for it, ready with a quip or a
blow, and ready with an ornery kind of patience as well. If he
sees I am depressed about something, he doesn't console; he
says, "Life is like a stone wall; let one stone start sliding and
you're done for! Well, good-by—and good luck!" I find this view
of life exhilarating.

I have never heard him say anything that did not come from
deep inside his own experience, and when he tells me to be patient and not to be in such a hurry, I take it because I know that
he has learned his own patience and his own rhythm through a
long life. In the years I have known him, he has taught me a
great deal. I have soaked him up like some healthy primal
source, and he has nourished the poet as well as the gardener.
He uses language like a poet himself, and savors his own pithy
turns of phrase, so they come back like recurring themes in a
fugue. One of my favorites is "He knows as much about farming

as a goose knows about Jesus."

What he talks about is often himself, himself as a legendary figure who inhabits the center of the myth, for he likes to look back on his life and ruminate on it. After seven years as a prison guard, he went back to farming, first working for richer men and then on his own, but wherever he was, whether master or servant, he must always have been enclosed in the armor of an immensely self-reliant and essentially solitary man. For he has chosen a kind of solitude even within his family. Joining a church would seem as ludicrous to him as joining any other sort of club. I haven't yet been able to persuade him to come to a Town Meeting. On Old Home Day in August, when the village gathers on the green for games, speeches, and a band concert, Perley Cole gets into his new blue pick-up and disappears. Last year he decided to revisit old haunts and pay a few calls on relatives in and near Cornish.

As usual after any expedition, he came round a few days later to tell me all about it in great detail. This time it was a saga of changing times. He told me how he sat in the Chevy and looked out on what remained of a rich farm where he had worked forty or more years ago, a farm of great silos and barns, of many acres of pasture and corn.

"It's a wilderness," he said. "It's all gone to pot, grown up into brush, barns fallen in or burned. I tell you if I had stayed there another five minutes, I'd have gone crazy!"

He stopped in Cornish to look up old acquaintances, talked to a man and named names.

"Brother," the man told him, "if you want to see any of them, you'll have to go to the cemetery!"

"You should never have left Nelson," I teased him. "Around here we're most of us alive."

That's how we talk, veering away from what is too painful to contemplate. But after he had left I thought over all he had said, and shivered as the shadow of death and decay passed over the house like a cloud. And then the sun came out as I felt in my bones the resilience of the old man, the way he himself has handled change, not by resisting it but by playing his own game within it.

In his late sixties, when he still had a herd of cows and it was becoming harder and harder to get help he could afford, he went through a period of black depression. "It got so as when I went into the barn and looked at all those cows, I sat down on a stool and wept!" The time had come to make a radical change, and unlike many a farmer who dies in harness, Perley had the wit to recognize that he had reached the limit. He and Angie said good-by to the cows and to Hillsboro and looked around for a little place where they could settle in, free of the anxieties and responsibilities of a working farm.

So it came about that they were brought to Nelson to look at the old place back of the schoolhouse. Angie, as he has often explained to me, has the last word about everything indoors but his word is law on anything outside the house. Nevertheless, I have noticed that she manages to sneak some flower seeds into the vegetable garden, and it was she, not he, who made the final decision on their house. Perley was not enthusiastic—I have never been able to find out why. At any rate they moved in. He was kept busy the first year sprucing up the old place. He spent the first winter on snowshoes tracking down hedgehogs (as the porcupine is called in New Hampshire). But by their second year, he no doubt began to feel pretty restless, especially as he keeps his eyes open and he could see how much needed doing all over the village. And so one day he appeared on my doorstep.

He might have been an apparition from another age, an age when a workman still had the time and the patience and the wish to do a patient, perfect job, not for the money, not even for the praise he might get at the end of the day, but out of self-respect and out of the love of the work for its own sake. In this Perley is very much like a poet, and he stands before me as an exemplar. Thinking of the way he kneels down to clip a border after he has cut the grass, I sometimes have revised a page for the fifth time instead of letting it go after the fourth. In fact I find that when he is on the place I work better. There he is somewhere off in the woods cutting brush, and here I am at my desk pruning out a thicket of words. It gives me a little extra zip to know he is there. It's both companionable, in a curious solitary way, and inspiring.

I can't imagine how I should ever have managed without him. Until very recently no friend has turned up here whose joy it is to work out of doors with me. If in those first years I had looked ahead to all that was to be done, to all that needed doing, I should have despaired. But little by little, together, Perley and I have lifted the place out of its neglect and chaos into something like beauty and order. Sometimes he surprises me with a job of his own invention. Last year when I came back from a semester away as Poet in Residence at a Midwestern college, I found that the barn, which had become a general dump for anything and everything, had been completely organized and tidied up. Garden stakes were tied into bundles according to size. Flowerpots were arranged in one corner, according to shape. A huge mass of odd lumber and two-by-fours left by the builders had been cut to kindling size and neatly stacked. Every tool had been cleaned and put into the best possible shape. Well, it was a glorious homecoming!

In these last years Perley has been getting rid of bracken and brush to clear out the whole hillside below the garden, and so set off the stone wall and the big trees at its foot. He has pruned out around a single birch, the only one I can see from the house, so that elegant white figure stands out at the end of one meadow. He has penetrated a small, ragged wood behind the barn and cleared it so that six small ash trees in lines of three now "finish" that end of the barn when I sit on the back porch on a summer evening. One fall he pruned along the stone wall that divides my property from the church grounds, so that too has shape and form at last. Little by little what was a derelict farm is becoming a small estate. We have a continuous joke about this, for when I have been away and come back, it is not unusual for Perley to tell me that "a man" stopped in a car and offered $100,000 for it. The sum grows each year, and with reason. My answer is, "I'm not selling!"

"Not for a hundred thousand?" Perley asks, lifting his eyebrows.

"Not for a million."

Perley's domain is the woods and fields; mine is the garden proper. For flowers are not his specialty and he knows next to nothing about them. Nevertheless it is he who comes to dig big holes for me when (and always unexpectedly) an order of bushes and plants arrives from a nurseryman. It is he who prunes the little fruit trees that I planted eight years ago and that have begun to bear at last. It is he who limes and rolls and cuts the lawns and trims the borders. It is he who goes out and cuts the spruce and hemlock to lay on the borders when I put them to bed in November. And when I am away, as I often have to be—when I go out on a teaching stint to help pay the bills, it is he who can be depended on to see that everything is well taken care of in my absence. Of all that Nelson has given me he is the pearl of great price.

But if Perley often resembles a guardian angel, the angel has two faces and one is less benign. He is a "good scrapper" he informs me, as if I didn't know! Every now and then he is seized on by a fury. I have thought about this a lot because I recognize the same symptoms in myself. Pressure of one kind or another builds up and finally blows itself off in anger. Once he walked off the place and did not come back for two days, leaving a job half finished. I called Angie, finally, to ask what the matter was.

"Oh, you know Perley," she said in her gentle voice. "I can't say, but he'll get over it."

"You tell him to come down here and have it out," I said.

Much to my surprise he did come down, prepared with a speech of considerable color and length which I suspect he had been rehearsing. He had come down to tell me to get a younger man, that he was through. It took some doing but I finally penetrated his meaning, which was that I had said at the end of the morning two days before, "You've been at it long enough, Perley." I am always slightly anxious for fear his passionate concern for the job will lead him to overdo. (The man is, after all, seventy-seven now.) Perley had taken my statement to mean that he had been *slow*, an old man not worth his pay! The court was in session and I listened. After I had listened, I persuaded him that if he went home and didn't come back the salt would lose its savor and nothing ever feel quite right again.

But if that storm blew over, there is always a new one in the air whenever Perley comes down with a bill. No one could possibly pay him enough for what he does, but for some reason he always behaves like a horse about to shy. There is a defiant look in his eye, as if he imagined the bill would be thrown in his face as exorbitant.

"Now if you don't want me around after this," he says, as if he had committed some crime, "there'll be no hard feelings. You'll always be welcome at our house."

By this time I'm as nervous as he is and prepared to pay out a fortune, considering what has been accomplished. He then hands me an itemized bill with every hour accounted for, and I am a-bashed to see how little it turns out to be after all. Why all this fuss?

Now and then the myth-making inner world swells up and floods all sense of reality. It is as if an enraged bear were loose inside Perley, and I have learned that it is best at such times to keep away. But the violence he directs against others, a violence of speech rather than action as I have known him, he sometimes directs against himself. Once when he confessed to uprooting a rare plant by mistake, he said, "I should be shot right through the heart!"

Perley's moods are rather like the New England weather, and, like the weather, he keeps me on my toes, for I never know what to expect. Sometimes he is in a mood to tease. When he learned that I had got a rifle to scare woodchucks off, he was delighted, and ever since has woven many a tall story around my imaginary exploits. "I hear so and so is in hospital, shot through the tail and groaning like a wounded bear," he will say, referring to an ornery local character with whom I have had words. "Looks like he won't live," Perley says, letting out a brief guffaw as he saunters off.

Am I wrong in believing that he is happier now than he has ever been? that finding a village that needed a lot of trimming up was just what he hankered after when the cows had gone? —not to mention his being cock of the walk in a village of old ladies, all of whom need his help. He does exactly what he pleases and when he pleases, knocks off at noon and takes a long nap, and sometimes decides to take a holiday for a week or so. "I'm going into my tunnel," he says, and vanishes until whatever he does in the tunnel has been accomplished. Lately Angie has been ill for a long time, away in a hospital, and he has taken to reading intensively. "I read and I meditate," he told me the other day, and added, "Meditation is like religion."

For a second I felt the phrase was out of character, but I have thought about it and I think that Perley, like all of us, is changing. In all those first years, he and I stood, as it were, outside time. Old? In a given day he did twice the work of most men of thirty. But in these last five years I have been learning that middle age is not youth. My work day is not as long as it used to be. And in these five years Perley has moved from what still felt like the prime of life when he was seventy to old age. I face the fact that he will not be with me forever. But when he tries to persuade me that he is through, we come to settle for "just one more year and then we'll see."

And it will still take a while to get us tidied up here in the village. There is nothing that pleases Perley more than to survey a tangled jungle of rotten trees and brush and to carve it into shape. Contemplating what would look to most of us like an impossible task, he begins to hum with anticipation; his face, often harsh in repose, lights up with the joy of battle, with the artist's joy. Hours later he emerges, his straw hat pulled down over his eyes, his shirt collar tucked in, and swallows a glass of sherry as if it were water. Behind him beauty and order have been restored.

When he and I are working side by side here, as we do, for a few hours anyway we are neither old nor young. We are outside time.

TEN

A Flower-Arranging Summer

MAKING A GARDEN is not a gentle hobby for the elderly, to be picked up and laid down like a game of solitaire. It is a grand passion. It seizes a person whole, and once it has done so he will have to accept that his life is going to be radically changed. There are seasons when he will hesitate to travel, and if he does travel, his mind will be distracted by the thousand and one children he has left behind, children who are always in peril of one sort or another. However sober he may have been before, he will soon become an inveterate gambler who cuts his losses and begins again; he may think he intends to pare down on spending energy and money, but that is an illusion, and he soon learns that a garden is an ever-expanding venture. Whatever he had considered to be his profession has become an avocation. His vo-

Photograph by Eleanor Blair

cation is his garden.

How lucky it is for me, then, that Nelson is far enough north so there are four months of the year when there is nothing to be done outdoors! By late November the garden has been put to bed and will sleep until late April. Snowbound, I can at last concentrate on writing. But when the day's stint is done I pore over seed catalogues and the brochures of nurserymen, and dream of next year's garden. So, at least in my imagination, the garden is very much alive all the time . . . as with any other grand passion.

When Céline and I planted those first perennials, I had no idea what I was getting myself in for, for I had never had a garden of my own. But I did recognize the symptoms of the vocation from living near my mother, who could not inhabit an apartment for even a few months without taking over a little plot of earth under a porch or alongside a back entrance and making it flower. It is an English trait, as anyone recognizes who has approached London by train and seen, behind each smoke-and-dirt-encrusted row of sad houses, the diversity of tiny gardens, each an expression of the personality of its lover and slave. It is an English trait as anyone knows who has seen a work of the imagination such as Vita Sackville-West's and Harold Nicholson's Sissinghurst, a garden that wonderfully combines the romantic vision within a classical frame, a garden like a series of hedge-enclosed rooms that lead from one to another, opening classic perspectives toward moments of romantic discovery. Who can forget a small corner of massed blue poppies against a low brick wall, or the tall fox lilies like plumes of smoke against a dark hedge?

The need to create gardens may be an English trait but it can be transplanted, as I knew when I first saw Marjorie Sedgwick's apparently casual planting of Chinese peonies under pink and white dogwood and Japanese maple in Beverly, Massachusetts. Her garden is an impressionist's dream of light flowing through petals, a garden full of surprises too, such as a square pool with pink lotus flowering in it, where least expected, on the rim of a steep decline.

It is absurd, of course, to place these serious works of art beside my "sample garden" here at Nelson. I called it a sample garden at first because I had to experiment to find out what would grow here, and also because I was not imagining it in large spaces or forms—the wilderness outside provides the perspective—but rather as a series of intimate gatherings of flowers, as in a Flemish tapestry, to be looked at one by one, and above all to be picked!

One cannot impose one's will on a garden; something has already been imposed, the terrain itself, the landscape in which it is to be created. The Japanese, of course, are the great masters of using and defining what has been given. When I came back from Japan, I saw every rock in my meadow with fresh eyes, the whole state of New Hampshire as a vast Japanese rock garden, where the wildness, the casualness, is the quality to be preserved. At the opposite extreme, the French rationalize nature, impose a geometric plan upon it, and use flowers as if they were pigment for large blocks and lines of color. Somewhere between the two lies the English garden, so much more flowery than the Japanese, so much more casual than the French. It was in the English genius to invent the herbaceous border, with its sequences following each other like phrases in music, from massed tulips, hyacinths, iris, and daffodils in the spring through all the changes to the last cloud of asters in late fall. The trick is to have something in flower all the time and always changing, so the big border becomes a slow-moving kaleidoscope, never quite the same from one week to the next. It is not an easy trick, as I have discovered, but it is an absorbing one to try to master, and, like everything else in a garden, even the failures become the food of dreams for "next year."

At Nelson the garden has made itself bit by bit as I enclose or shape or push back a little more of the wilderness. What I had to play with was broken-down stone walls, some rough spaces of open lawns punctuated by rough granite boulders, and a classic early-nineteenth-century façade, the house itself. At first

I worked with what was there, the two front borders and the sunken place in the foundations of the old barn. As time went on I found myself wanting more than anything to frame what I had by clearing out small growth. It is almost unbelievable what giving a garden space to breathe in will do. The first great operation of this kind was to cut out the small trees and brush below the terrace, and clear it to the stone wall at the boundary. The two Quigley boys worked at this on two heroic days one September, and carted off truckload after truckload of little trees. When I saw the result, I felt I had suddenly acquired not a ragged garden but a small estate. The two endeavors, to open up and to define or frame by means of boundary—a wall, a building, a line of trees, or even a single bush—go together. They are what make the big design. Up a level from the terrace, it is the barn that helps to frame the big plot of annuals. After Perley came I extended the terraced garden by one level, cutting out a lot of wild raspberry to make a piece of lawn and a narrow flower bed against a few yards of "defining" picket fence.

But the first thing was to break up the rather stark façade of the house with a few lilac bushes, and to use others—viburnum, rugosa roses, and such—to make bold shapes among the beds of flowers. The lovely beauty bush, like a pale-pink cloud, has done especially well. I also planted a small orchard of dwarf fruit trees at the back between house and barn, so that area looks less bare.

As to flowers, I wanted a garden for indoors as much as for outdoors; I wanted to have the materials for a succession of mixed bunches in the house all through the seasons. (If someone asked me what my idea of luxury is, I think my answer would be: flowers in the house all year round.) My outdoor garden would never win a ribbon from a garden club, but the indoor-outdoor garden has been a constant joy from the very first year. There are gardeners who cannot bear to pick. I am not one of them, so it has been a boon to have that plot at the back, a kind of kitchen garden, stuffed with lettuce and annuals that I can plunder without a qualm.

From May on, I can hardly wait to get up to see what has happened overnight, for one of the pleasures of a garden is that something is always happening; it is not static, even for a day. I go out by six-thirty and sometimes earlier, still in my pajamas and a wrapper, to take a look around before breakfast. Perhaps the hummingbird has come back and I'll catch a glimpse of the ruby throat as he flashes past and, like me, pauses at each flower. It sometimes seems as if each plant had its bird. The goldfinches love cosmos; the cedar waxwings too. The hummingbird is a great delphinium-drinker, and when that is gone stays on as long as nicotiana is in flower.

This early morning walk around the garden is contemplative. It is not a time to work but rather a time to taste the air, and not only to look at the flowers but to look out beyond the tamed world to the long meadow and the great trees beyond it, for they too are always changing. A most delightful thing about this garden is the wilderness it lies in, a small orderly pocket in a vast natural world. The present cats—two speckled sisters—sense the difference just as I do. Beyond the garden they creep in and out of the long grasses and among the daisies like tigers, but as soon as one of them is inside the garden proper, she comes to sit decorously under a rosebush, paws tucked in and wearing the expression of Queen Victoria at her most bland.

How much hope, expectation, and sheer hard work goes into the smallest success! There is no being sure of anything except that whatever has been created will change in time, and sometimes quite erratically. And, like parents whose children suddenly shoot up beyond them, I am always being taken by surprise. Those peonies in the big border are huge now, bearing perhaps fifty swanlike flowers each. But they have crowded out smaller plants. When the iris is at its most splendid, an army of white, gold, purple, and blue standards, the wary gardener knows that it is time to divide it. What is to be done with the basketfuls left over?

It never crossed my mind when I started that one of the joys would be to have plants to give away. But now two or three neighbors' gardens have flowered to new richness on my iris. In exchange I have been given lovely bits of theirs—a white rugosa rose that Mildred dug up for me one day; the loveliest lilac I have, deep purple, that Quig brought over early one morning and laid beside my back steps. I set it in right there, and there, every spring, it flowers in Quig's name.

The first half hour of the morning I spend enjoying the air and watching for miracles. After breakfast I spend an hour or more arranging and rearranging seven or eight bunches of flowers for the house. There are flowers indoors here all the year around—in winter, bowls of narcissus, geraniums brought in from the windowboxes in the autumn, cut flowers from a local florist when all else fails. But from late May on I have variety to play with, and the joy becomes arduous and complex. Arranging flowers is like writing in that it is an art of choice. Not everything can be used of the rich material that rushes forward demanding utterance. And just as one tries one word after another, puts a phrase together only to tear it apart, so one arranges flowers. It is engrossing work, and needs a fresh eye and a steady hand. When you think the thing is finished, it may suddenly topple over, or look too crowded after all, or a little meager. It needs one more note of bright pink, or it needs white. White in a bunch of flowers does a little of what black does in a painting, I have found. It acts as a catalyst for all the colors. After that first hour I have used up my "seeing energy" for a while, just as, after three hours at my desk, the edge begins to go, the critical edge.

One of the things gardening does for me is to provide a way of resting without being bored; a day divided between writing in the morning and gardening in the afternoon has a good balance; it is possible to maintain what might be called perfect pitch, total awareness, for a good many hours of such a day. And gardening is so rich in sensuous pleasures that I hardly notice its solitariness.

Flowers and plants are silent presences; they nourish every sense except the ear . . . and that subtle observer Elizabeth

McClelland once wrote of the "creaking" of the tulips, so even hearing may be involved. What a pleasure it is to touch the hairy bud of a poppy, or to pick up the velvety fallen petal of a rose, or to get a wave of sharp sweetness from the peony bed as one goes past! One cannot eat these glories, but I often pick a raspberry or two while I am working, or chew a mint leaf or a sprig of parsley. Plants do not speak, but their silence is alive with change.

For the joys a garden brings are already going as they come. They are poignant. When the first apple falls with that tremendous thud, one of the big seasonal changes startles the heart. The swanlike peony suddenly lets all its petals fall in a snowy pile, and it is time to say good-by until another June. But by then the delphinium is on the way, and the lilies . . . the flowers ring their changes through a long cycle, a cycle that will be renewed. That is what the gardener often forgets. To the flowers we never have to say good-by forever. *We* grow older every year, but not the garden; it is reborn every spring.

Like any grand passion, my garden has been nourished by memory as well as by desire, and is a meeting place, an intersection, where remembered joys can be re-created. I first saw shirley poppies—and if I had to choose only one flower, I might choose them—in Basil de Selincourt's garden near Oxford, in the Cotswolds. Basil sowed shirley poppies on a long bank a little above a more formal perennial border; and when they flowered, a diaphanous host, shaken by the light and wind, playing their endless variations on the themes of pink, white, and red, they were a wonder to behold. Everything about this flower is magic —its curious hairy stem; the tightly folded petals, a little damp, that open out of nothing like Fortuny dresses, to show the shaggy crown of gold or black stamens; and finally the intricate turret of the seed pod. So when my shirley poppies flower, it is Basil who comes back with them.

I first saw fritillaries—the flower, not the butterfly—by a brook at Penns in the Rocks, where the poet Dorothy Wellesley lived. The house took its name from a miniature mountain of wild rocks and trees near where it stands, in a hollow, as if they were both sunk in dream, as was the poet herself in her old age. There the ghost of Yeats was never very far away, the atmosphere all of legend as one climbed up to a small Grecian temple built in his memory at the top of the hill. The fritillaries broke into this dreamlike visit into the past with their vivid present. Could they be real, these tiny lanterns, chequered purple and white, opening to a bell with as sharply chiseled petals as in a child's drawing of an imaginary flower? They *were* real, and now they spring up here under an old forsythia bush, year by year, to evoke Yeats and D. W.—as if I should ever forget them!

Two Chinese peonies speak to me always of Ellery Sedgwick, being wheeled out in his last years to sit and contemplate one after another of these beauties, an old man whose exuberant delight flew out from him as if it were a flotilla of butterflies, to rest on this flower or that—a winged *attention* he gave also to those he loved, to poetry, to creation itself. Ellery, I miss you! But I find you again every June when the peonies are in flower.

My mother's light ghost is everywhere in my garden, of course, but there are certain times and certain places where I am more aware of her presence than usual. One time is October when I am on my knees for hours planting bulbs on every sunny day, for this was one task I often helped her with, the silver-gray cat, Cloudy, playing wildly among the leaves beside us, and the whole atmosphere one of hope. At the moment of planting a bulb, all is hope, no dismay. Then, there is surely something hauntingly symbolic about burying a living thing toward a sure resurrection, at a moment in the season when everything else is dying or on the way out. I order bulbs extravagantly, as I now know that more than half will make a chipmunk's winter bearable. But no matter what the casualties, in October the vision of massed tulips and daffodils is there in the mind's eye.

In the middle of the garden at Channing Place there was a patch of "wild wood," and here my mother planted trillium and bluebells. I was inspired to do the same in a patch of "wild wood" below the terraced gardens after Ruth Harnden came up from Plymouth with pink lady's-slippers from her woods and planted them there in my absence. Her gift suggested a new place to "expand" into. So last year I planted a hundred blue-bells down there. Will they spread, and eventually make a blue pool in memory of Mabel Sarton? Who knows? A garden is a perpetual experiment. It may evoke, but it can rarely memorialize, at least in the sense of imitation. Gardens are as original as people.

My mother is most with me as a living presence when I go out to weed. What better way to get over a black mood than an hour of furious weeding! That violent tearing up and casting away of the dreadfully healthy weeds also tears up and casts away the dreadfully healthy demons—and my mother had her demons too. Clearing away all that stifles and distresses tender plants to give them air and space clears away at the same time all that has been stifling the person. How often I have seen my mother come in from such a battle flushed with joy. There, in her garden, she balanced a rich and sometimes anguished temperament against tough reality, and there, she, so frail in some ways, plagued by illness, learned how to survive.

Yes, gardening gives one back a sense of proportion about everything except itself. What a relief it was to me when I read that Vita Sackville-West kept a pile of metal labels in a shed at Sissinghurst as proof of all the experiments that had failed! I had, until then, been ashamed of how much waste there was even in my unpretentious garden here. I blamed inexperience, impatience, and extravagance. But now I have come to accept that one must not count the losses, they would be too alarming. One must count only the joys, and feel continually blessed in them. There is no unlucky gardener, for each small success so heavily outweighs each defeat in his passionate heart.

Two years ago, the dwarf plum trees by the kitchen door flowered for the first time. Is there a more haunting presence than plum? It is sweet, but not too sweet, a little spiced, sweetness with a shade of bitterness in it. I remember getting out of the train at Enka-Kuji, a Zen monastery not far from Tokyo, on a chill March day, and being taken by surprise. What was that incense? It was plum blossom.

Now it was here, right at my door. I could look out on two clouds of white, supported on black irregular twigs, and alive with bees. The next morning the oriole came to shine his orange flame among all those white petals. I could hardly believe it. I had heard the oriole more than once, but I had not actually seen one since that first day when I came to look at the house and he had appeared on the maple like an angel. Yes, it was true. The oriole had come back to celebrate the first flowering of the plum, and perhaps also to celebrate much else that had seemed wild dream and has come true in the last six years.

Is there a joy except gardening that asks so much, and gives so much? I know of no other except, perhaps, the writing of a poem. They are much alike, even in the amount of waste that has to be accepted for the sake of the rare, chancy joy when all goes well. And they are alike in that both are passions that bring renewal with them. But there is a difference: poetry is for all ages; gardening is one of the late joys, for youth is too impatient, too self-absorbed, and usually not rooted deeply enough to create a garden. Gardening is one of the rewards of middle age, when one is ready for an impersonal passion, a passion that demands patience, acute awareness of a world outside oneself, and the power to keep on growing through all the times of drought, through the cold snows, toward those moments of pure joy when all failures are forgotten and the plum tree flowers.

ELEVEN

Death and the Maple

IT HAD NOT OCCURRED TO ME until lately that a house is warmed by death as well as by life. But one day an English friend of mine, brought up in a house that had held many births and many deaths within its sheltering walls, and who had married an American and come to live in his exquisite new house, said, "Yes, it is beautiful. But I shall never feel at home in this house because no one has died here." My walls hold the death of "Aunt Cora." I do not brood about it, but I am not unaware that she died here in my study, a frail hunchback who had never been "downed" by a very hard life, and that death is a part of the human richness, the truth of the house for me.

We can accept death. It is dying that is not and never will be acceptable. For us who have to witness dying, it must always feel as if the very fabric of life were being torn apart. I was to experience that cruel tearing two years after I moved in, and in a strange way.

The great maple where the oriole had burst into song on that first day in May was beginning to show the signs of extreme old age. Standing between the house and the wide meadow that separates my grounds from the churchyard, it had looked at first as if it would live forever. It was such a staunch tree, wide at the base, branching low, so it rose up in amplitude, making a wide arc against the sky, "the great tree" of the place. But spring by spring a few more branches failed to leaf out, and in winter it had begun to groan when the icy north winds tore at it. More than once I got up in the night and paced the floor to shut out that sound, the wrenching, long creak and shudder, so much like suffering. What if the huge trunk did crack and the tree crash against the house? I was not alone in my anxiety. Neighbors looked up at it and shook their heads. "Sooner or later that tree will have to come down. It's a risk." Yes, sooner or later. . . . I put off the decision because it felt like murder.

But one summer day a truck stopped in the road, two young men got out, knocked at my door, and offered to take it down and cut and stack the wood for fifty dollars. Well, they had come, the messengers of fate, and I made the decision on the spot. But I was not going to watch. I went back to my desk to work, or to try to work. I had not imagined what that day would be like.

The men first got busy with a buzz saw, cutting into the enormous trunk, four feet across at least, representing over a hundred years of growth. Is there a more nerve-racking sound than the hideous, mechanistic screech of a buzz saw at work? It is an anti-sound. It does not fit in with any landscape or with any state of mind, except possibly hatred in its most dehumanized form. Under any circumstances I find the sound hard to bear; that day it was worse, for the saw was slicing into the living trunk of my tree. I could not look.

But when at last there was silence again, a long silence, I

turned around to find out what was happening behind my back. I watched the men drive their truck far out into the meadow, then come back on foot to attach a heavy rope, first around the massive trunk of the tree, and then around the truck, for the *coup de grace*. I had to go outside. Quig was there, watching from his front yard, but we did not call or even wave to each other. It was a moment filled with awe. We watched in silence as the two men, for whom no doubt this was just "another job," got into the truck, started the motor, and inched forward until the rope was taut.

The saw had cut into the trunk more than halfway, and it should have been a simple matter now to pull that towering strength down. But we had to stand and watch the truck struggle, in short lunges, give up, and then start again, over and over. I felt the sweat on my face, for it was clear that the tree was not going to make it easy for anyone. The struggle was silent, and that made it all the worse. The tree was fighting for its life; it did not want to go.

After repeated attempts the men shut off the motor, got down from the truck, and soon the angry saw started up again. It had become a grim business. I went indoors, finding the suspense unbearable. But the end had to come soon, and it did. When the trunk tore apart, I was not watching. I heard a harsh crack, and then a kind of sigh as the branches sank through the air, and it was over. At last it was over.

There is no comfort when a great tree goes. There is no comfort in the dying struggle. For many months I missed something in the air over my head . . . that branch high up where once the oriole sang. But when winter came, I found comfort in those maple logs burning on a hearth. There are worse ways to die.

That was the first death that came to Nelson, to me. It was followed by a human death that cut closer to the marrow. In late autumn I began to notice that Quig, although he still came over sometimes to sit by the fire, refused anything to eat, and only sipped his drink "for the sake of the ceremony." At that time he was engrossed in a tremendous job on his house; he had opened

up two rooms to make a single big living room, and was engaged now in building on a whole new end. He was doing this
alone, with occasional help from the boys, and it was a great
deal to ask of himself, a man nearly seventy, so I thought at first
that what he showed was extreme fatigue. He complained of not
feeling well, and sometimes laid down his tools for a bit, the job
half done. But he rallied when an important commission came
his way, to paint the portraits of four boys in Keene. This demanded an intensity that carpentry does not. What a supreme
effort the artist must have called out of himself, to summon his
skill, his concentration, for one last time, to put that commission
through! Somehow he did it, and only when the four portraits
were finished did he admit to himself and to us that he was seriously ill.

I have come to believe that the way people die expresses the
central person as clearly as the way they have lived or the way
they have loved. My mother, as I accompanied her through long
months of a gradual waning, never once complained or begged
to be released from pain; she seemed to fold herself inward like
a closing flower, to detach herself gently from all she had loved,
to "let go," until she seemed to us to have become nothing but
light, an impersonal light, as if there were nothing left for death
to take but the soul itself.

The outwardness of Jean Dominique's last years was certainly tragic: she had seen her two life companions die and, as
her eyes failed, had had to depend on the care of strangers. But
those last years were so shot through by imagination, fantasy,
the extraordinary charm of the being who suffered and enjoyed
within them, that the word "tragic" becomes inappropriate. Out
of nothing, Jean Dominique was still making everything, as she
had seventy years before when she had suffered a period of
blindness as a little girl and wrote of herself and her father, "Together they breathed deeply, like people who exaggerate their
soul because they have no other riches." Every layer of pride
and reserve was peeled off one by one, until what was left was
nothing but a translucent center, as alive to light and shadow, to

a caress, to a passing bird, as is a child or a very old woman of genius.

Katrine Greene, so much younger, died in the splendor of unremitting battle, would not accept the sentence when it came, used every ruse, every weapon her intelligence could muster to keep her life alive, lived with such intensity as she died that she could lift death up like a glass of champagne and drink it down "To Life!"

As theirs had been, Quig's dying was in character—as casual, as human and perceptive as his every gesture. Much of the time he preferred to sit up in an armchair; he was full of jokes. And it seemed for awhile as if he were being given an Indian summer just before the end, although I can say this only looking back. No one realized that he was dying, and perhaps he didn't know it himself. He had always lived in amazing hopefulness on the edge of nowhere.

But now there began to be pain. He and Mildred sat up far into the night playing cribbage to try to help him forget it. In the daytime he was distracted by visitors, who came, one by one, to sit and talk as they had always done, to chaff him a little; he listened attentively, as he had always done, a gleam of mischief in his eye. With the dog Honey at his feet, he resembled an old chieftain surrounded by his clan, those who came to pay respects and often stayed to be comforted. The only way we knew that he must be seriously ill was that he no longer spoke of projects. Quietly he had laid aside paints, the gold leaf for the frames, even his violin, though he liked to have it near him. If the big room was only half finished, at least it was closed in against the rain. He had done what he could.

Quig may have complained of pain during those days when it got really bad, but he never complained of life. His eyes still lit up at the word "France" or at the name of Alec James; he recalled the early days of his marriage when he and Mildred had walked all over the world as far as their legs could take them on a Sunday—and how that had once been thirty miles. . . . No, we could not believe that Quig was dying.

But in the middle of January he went into hospital, the Keene hospital where his three children had been born; there the X-rays showed advanced cancer, beyond the operable stage. Mildred went in every day to be with him, and sometimes I was the friend to drive her. So it happened that I looked around for something to take him, and picked a volume of Delacroix's journal out of the bookcase—a small, light book, for it was printed on India paper, and I thought he could hold it without too great an effort. His face was hollow, but his eyes shone as he grasped the little book, and opened it, by chance, to the stunning portrait of Chopin. Then there was silence while Quig disappeared into his world of joy, the world of the painter, lost in a "fit of looking." That was my last sight of him.

Quig had been so much a part of this landscape that we had come to take him for granted like some sturdy deep-rooted tree that would surely outlive us all. Then, quite suddenly, he was not there, leaving a huge empty space in the air, as my old maple had done after it was cut down.

Death frames the essential. What was framed for us on that final day is hard to put into words, elusive. Perhaps what we mourned was a whole man. All the fragments of a life that had sometimes seemed to scatter itself among too many gifts came together, and we saw him whole. And we began to see what the wholeness was all about—a capacity for pure joy, a capacity for tenderness rarely seen in a man. It was the human triumph of one who had tasted almost no worldly success but who had never ceased to create and to give. I never went out with Quig without seeing something I had not noticed before—I remember, for instance, his pointing out how much red there is among the feathery greens of spring. I never talked with him without feeling that I had learned something of moment.

Strange, how much can be summed up in a little tale. But after his death I kept going back to one of his tales and pondering on it as if it held a clue. It had happened when he was working on the night shift at the woolen mill during the Depression. Among his fellow workers there was an old man from Nova

Scotia who heard that Quig knew the jigs and reels of the old time and could play them. The old man begged Quig to bring his violin and play for him at the coffee break, and finally Quig did so, although he had been warned that the old man might want to dance and that he had a weak heart. Well, it was a chance you took for the sake of life. They went down to an empty room under the factory, and Quig swung into that music irresistible to the feet of an old folk-dancer. The old man was taken by a fit of gaiety, and, once his toe was tapping, there was no stopping him. He danced his way up and down the floor like a boy in love. But the time was up, and Quig ran up the stairs to get back on his shift. Only later that day he was told that the time had really been up—that the old man had dropped dead as he climbed the stairs. Was it joy? was it grief that Quig felt when he told that story? Hard to know, but I have an idea it was joy. It is something to have given an old man his heart's desire just before he died.

I was so full of all this on the morning of Quig's death that I sat down and wrote what I felt, wrote quickly, almost as one makes a death mask, to catch the total being before the winds disperse it. What came out of that moment of acute feeling is, perhaps, not a work of art, but it is a celebration. As a celebration it served. *The Keene Sentinal* published it on the editorial page, and the minister read it at the funeral instead of the words he had brought with him. Being useful in this way, feeling that for once I could serve an immediate need as a poet, here among my neighbors, was a great comfort. It set a seal on my relation to the community. I had been "taken in." So, in a way, the poem was Quig's last gift to me.

That was January 24th, 1961, almost exactly six years ago. But I don't suppose a day passes when I am here in Nelson that I do not think of him for one reason or another. When I lie down for a short rest after lunch in the cosy room, my eyes rest on one of his paintings, a memory of Maine, a rather somber scene of early-morning fishermen setting up a net, the colors dark grays and browns. It is a painting that drinks light. On a gray day it is all a smouldering darkness, but in sunlight the water comes alive, those slate blues and grays suddenly shine. I have found it a good painting to live with because it is always changing. I think of Quig every time I open the cupboard door in the *bahut* to take out a glass, for when the hinge broke in two, he mended it for me. I think of him when the first reds come out among the feathery greens of spring; I think of him when his lilac flowers in rich purple plumes.

But as time goes on we not only remember specific things in relation to the people we have loved; their lives get built into our lives and finally the transference is complete. We are what we are because of them. When I am getting very dogmatic, I sometimes hear Jean-Do's amused voice saying very gently, "Pourquoi avoir raison?" "Why have to be right?" I am more aware now than I was during his life of how much Quig's friendship, his very existence even apart from our own relationship, did to help me forge out the position of these last years about my work. It is good for a professional to be reminded that his professionalism is only a husk, that the real person must remain an amateur, a *lover* of the work. Whatever we do well is done spontaneously for its own sake, in just the way Quig suddenly decided that he had to get up to the schoolhouse room and paint, or, equally spontaneously, had to make muffins! I am, I think, more of a poet than I was before I knew him, if to be a poet means allowing life to flow through one rather than forcing it to a mold the will has shaped; if it means learning to let the day shape the work, not the work, the day, and so live toward essence as naturally as a bird or a flower.

TWELVE

Learning about Water

FROM THE BEGINNING I had a special feeling about my well. It is built into one end of the porch beside the kitchen, like a round buried tower. When Earle made a new cover for it, he scratched my name into the cement, as well as the date when I had signed the deed, June 7th, 1958. Forty feet below, three sources brought me sweet, cold water, water that proved, when I had it tested in Concord, to be as pure as it tasted. Drawing on my own well added something to my sense of the house as an ark and a refuge in time of trouble. It became a rite to drink a glass from it whenever I had been away and came back. I was a well-owner!

Of course no well is inexhaustible. I showed my city-bred ignorance the first summer by setting up a whirling lawn hose and letting it run all day, and then being very much dismayed when

Photograph by Eleanor Blair

the water ran out. "It's a good well, fed by three sources," Mrs. Rundlett had told me; in the old days it had taken care of a barnful of cows and horses and had never gone dry. Now, within twenty-four hours it filled up again, and I had learned my first lesson, a lesson about time. A well is an ancient thing and an electric pump is a modern one; the pump marches to a different tempo. The well may be forty feet deep, but the motion of its rising is very gentle.

I still had much to learn. In 1961 we had a dry summer. It proved to be the beginning of a cycle, which is still not completed, although, perhaps luckily, we did not at first realize what we were in for. That cycle is now in its fifth year, and even city people, as far south as New York, are learning what lack of water means, and not to waste it.

By the third summer I had to be careful even when taking the hose from plant to plant by hand, and never watering the whole garden at the same time. Every morning I woke to scan the sky for the mercy of a cloud, but there it was, again and always, the implacable burning blue overhead. At the bank in Keene I heard that farmers in the region were selling out; it was hard enough to find water now for the cows, but even worse, the newly planted corn was shriveling before it grew more than a foot tall, so there would be no fodder either, come August. Sometimes it is comforting to realize that one is not alone before a scourge, but when a whole region begins to dry out, it is difficult not to feel panic. I remembered then with nostalgia the rain dances of the Pueblo Indians, the fervor of those dances under an equally implacable sky, and, so often, the blessed coming of the rain as if in answer to prayer. Here in New England each of us was alone; we had no such communal ways to seek for help. All we could do was wait and hope.

Every now and then Perley came over at my request to slide the heavy cement cover off the well and fling down a long pole at the end of a rope to measure the depth of the water.

"Well," he said one day, "you still have six feet."

Six feet between me and—what?

A few weeks later, the word was "four," then "two," and by then the water was muddy. I had long since given up flushing the toilet more than once a day (we forget in our extravagance that one flush uses five gallons!), but I could not stand and watch the garden die. I went on watering, after sunset, a little at a time, hoping to revive what looked most wilted. But quick shallow watering hardly helps deep-rooted perennials and may actually do harm; it does keep annuals alive, as well as cucumbers and zucchini, the great fleshy leaves of which may droop in a pitiful way by noon but revive again if given a small drink. I felt responsible, as if the garden had become a host of pleading children, and I who had given them life had fallen under a curse. To an absurd extent I was aware of the thirst all around me.

Then the day came when I had used up the small reserve in the well. I heard the repeated awful gasping as pressure was set up and the pump pumped in vain. Where had those three sources gone?

If I had reached the end of my tether, Perley was still resourceful. He hauled over a sixty-gallon tank from his barn, set it up on trestles in front of the house, and kept it filled for me from a spring three miles away.

In time of drought, the word "spring" is like a cool pebble in the mouth. In that huge dry world, it seemed like a miracle that there was still, a few miles down the road, a place where water flowed freely, cool pure water that sprang from under an immense boulder at the top of a hill and slipped down through moss and fallen leaves to pour itself into a hollowed-out granite trough. Such a source takes one right back into mystery, into the beginnings of our world, to the Old Testament itself. The farmer who carved the long hollow into the rock, and hauled it with two teams of oxen from miles away to set it there by the road for all the thirsty, whether animal or man, was mindful of this. On its side, he had carved out the words "My strength cometh from the hills."

For months there was hardly a time in daylight when someone was not there, filling up bottles and cans to take home in his car, and it was wonderful to see the basin replenished again and again from the inexhaustible source. I noticed that Perley, a man from another time, with different standards from most of us, was the only one to clean out the trough when he came, and to keep it clean, and to pick up the cigarette butts and cartons and beer bottles that others, less sensitive to the communion we shared, had left strewn about.

All through that hard time I leaned on Perley's strength, on his power to endure and not to panic. And his dour "Well, it's the worst I've ever seen" had a grain of comfort in it. We could not, then, be expected to take the catastrophe with philosophic calm. But we could face it together. "Two heads are better than one," he was fond of reminding me with a twinkle in his eye, "especially when one is a sheep's head."

Whichever one of ours is the sheep's head (and I fear it is mine) we came to the same conclusion at about the same time. There is a limit to "making do." Even with sixty gallons to spend, I had to count every drop. Nothing ever felt really clean any more. I used as few dishes as I could, and went swimming when I needed a bath. This penury was irritating but endurable. Worse was to have to witness nature, my own garden and the whole world around me, shriveling up. There are people in the world who, day after day, cannot give their children enough to eat, who watch them getting thinner and thinner, people who endure this, day after day, year after year. I know what they feel, or something of what they feel.

Water, like food, is essential. The lack of it breaks down one's faith in life itself. I looked up now at the tallest trees and imagined that the leaves were withering before they could turn. The grass in the meadow was tinder-dry. The fear of fire is never very far away from us in summer; no one will ever forget the year when half of Maine went up in smoke and Mount Desert was left a black wasteland. All of my neighbors have, at least once, gone out day after day, sometimes for twenty hours at a stretch, to beat out forest fire. And still the relentless blue skies never changed, as if some primary motion of the air had been stilled forever. I grew to hate the sun, to wait impatiently for the dark, when at least I could not see the withered flowers.

Even Perley had reached the limit of what he could do. There was nothing for it, we agreed, but to drill for artesian water. It is a serious decision to make at best because there is no possible way of knowing ahead what the operation will cost. For a retired farmer, as for a poet, the risk had to be measured against growing desperation.

We made our decision at the same time, in the autumn of 1964, but by then well-drillers were in great demand, "as scarce as hens' teeth." Perley had his water before winter; I was still waiting.

The year 1964 is not one I shall ever forget, for it held a full measure of disaster of several kinds. I was not teaching that year; I had asked for a leave of absence from my lectureship at Wellesley College so that I could do a piece of difficult, sustained work. It was a novel, one I had pondered for a long time, and it was difficult because the theme itself—the sources of inspiration for a woman artist—roused more than usual anxiety, and involved weeding out all self-indulgence and wishful thinking to take a penetrating look at a kind of experience most people choose to bury. By late October, badgered by the drought, put off by the well-drillers for the time being, and engaged in the last nerve-racking revision on the book, I had accepted Elizabeth Ames's kind invitation to spend six weeks at Yaddo, that haven for writers and artists in Saratoga Springs. I had imagined that month of November as a time of concentrated work in peace, a fruitful respite from the concerns of Nelson. Instead, I would have to face there, alone, two hard blows which struck at the center of my life.

From Yaddo the novel had gone off to my agent, and there I received a letter from him that advised me not to try to publish it, *Mrs. Stevens Hears the Mermaids Singing.* My agent not only is the best of agents, but has become, over the years, a true friend. How could I not believe him? The pause between the completion of a work and its first reading by an impersonal eye is mined with self-questioning and doubt at best. But I had counted on the advance to carry me through the spring; writing the book had been a gamble in every way, and it looked as if I had to face the hard fact that I had lost.

I was still shaken by this blow when another one fell, and from an unexpected quarter. It was a brief letter from Wellesley's president to inform me that the English Department had decided to end our informal arrangement and I would not be re-appointed. True, the college owed me nothing; I had come in for a semester at a time to teach two seminars in creative writing. I had greatly enjoyed these sessions of teaching and the respite from total insecurity that they had given me; I loved the students; I had every reason to believe that the enrichment was mutual. The abrupt dismissal came as a real shock; I could hardly take it in at first. It shook me in an area where I have far more confidence in my powers than I have ever had in myself as a writer. What had gone wrong? I shall never know.

Because of these two letters, a strange conjunction that touched the central person so deeply, the last ten days of my stay at Yaddo were among the most baffled and depressed that I have ever experienced. For the moment there was nothing to be done but live through them as best I could. I did suggest to my agent that he let my publishers take a look at the novel. There was a faint, but very faint, hope in my mind that they might disagree with his verdict.

If the years of drought had brought on a kind of animal panic, the helplessness of the animal before powers he cannot control, these two blows created panic of another kind, even harder to deal with. A total lack of security about the future is easily surmounted by the arrogance and the resilience of youth —after all, then, nothing seems final. But I was fifty. It had taken me twenty years to build, between writing and teaching, a viable structure for my life. Now I struggled against the fear that the structure had collapsed, and that I must start once more from scratch.

There was only one way to do it, and that was to try to go deep enough under present catastrophe to the one mode of being, and the one true act, which no word from outside could ever deny me, to the place from which poetry springs, and perhaps most truly when one has been stripped down to what feels like nothingness. I wrote four poems before I left Yaddo. They helped. And the very great kindness of the atmosphere, as it is daily re-created by Elizabeth Ames, helped too, helped me over the first worst state of shock.

Curiously enough the weather also helped, for in those last days Yaddo became a Wagnerian scene—the scene of a glorious, destructive, and terrifying ice storm. All one night I listened to the sharp split and crash of enormous pines, one even falling in through a window in the library downstairs. I woke to a dazzling world, a world of cut glass, broken up by sunlight and refracting it like a prism. Bodies of trees lay around like glittering ruins on some silent stage, and Yaddo, that day, though a terrible sight, was glorious. The violent mood of the storm, followed by this catharsis of surpassing beauty, acted like a purge on my own violent mood.

I left despair behind me as I set out for home through the strange, altered world, all enclosed in ice. It was even exhilarating to get lost, as I did after I had crossed the Hudson. When I stopped to ask a telephone crew where I was, they laughed and said they had no idea. Crews had been sent into New York from other states, and we were all lost that day in a glittering nowhere. I enjoyed the rare strangeness of the landscape, and I enjoyed nursing the car along on very slippery roads . . . it was good to be active after the static state of shock, to be doing something as practical as finding the road, and to be slowly getting nearer to the kennel where I had left the cats. I was so anxious to see them, and to be back again myself in my own lair! Would the well-drillers perhaps have arrived? They had promised to be there within the week.

I have interrupted my tale of water with a long digression because the context in which I drilled for artesian water explains

why it became such a harrowing experience. Of course I was delighted to see the two men when they finally arrived—weeks
later—though their battered old truck and prehistoric-looking
equipment were not exactly reassuring. On the other hand, when
I had hired them I was solvent, with a new book on the fire and
a job to take up again in the autumn. Now things were different.
So my anxiety was very real as I watched them making their
preparations.

The rusty, dilapidated equipment, a kind of tower containing
a weighted turbine, was set upon the back of the truck. The ancient motor would supply power to drive it up and down,
through three or four feet of ice and snow, frozen earth, rocks,
Heaven knows what impediments. This part of the operation
was made more difficult because of extreme cold, nine below
zero one morning. The men were genial fellows, rather lazy and
not, I suspected, very competent, but they were there and I must
wait and see. It cannot be said that I was calm. I kept remembering Maurie's horrendous tale of her own well when it was
dug; they went four hundred feet and still had not struck water,
while she had watched her small savings vanish into that dry
hole. Finally she had to make a decision, to go on a few feet
deeper and trust her luck or to give up. She asked the question
on her knees, decided to chance one more try, and a few moments later they struck water. What was ahead of me? For it
was entirely possible that we might go four hundred feet (at
seven dollars a foot!) and not strike it even then!

I was not lucky in the rig that fate had provided; for once
the guardian angel had been busy somewhere else. The rig was
ancient and vulnerable, and broke down, it seemed, every day.
Then the men would go off for hours at a time to find a part, or
to eat a meal, or simply because they were discouraged. It
snowed again, so they couldn't work, or it was too cold. Sometimes they disappeared for several days, leaving me to contemplate the prehistoric monster in front of the house and the filthy
black mud that had welled up around and below it, mud that
looked like lava and ran down in thick black ooze toward a

rugosa bush I had planted at the edge of the lawn.

When, after days of absence, the drillers did come back, I listened hour after hour to the relentless sound of the piston as it was driven up and down, up and down, making the earth shudder, and hitting each time with a loud, dead thud that had something violent and sinister about it. The image that stayed with me all those days was of rape, a rape of the earth, a rape of something that resisted. Could lovely clear water ever be reached by such a brutal process?

Then, one morning, the stout, friendly young man who bossed the outfit knocked at the door to tell me that they had struck a boulder and would have to use dynamite to get through. Would it be safe? I asked. (They were drilling only ten feet from the house.) He assured me that they would take every precaution, and, as evidence, brought out an old mattress they intended to stuff into the mouth of the hole. What he did not tell me, as he went cheerfully off that day, was that he was about to buy—out of ignorance, I presume—about ten times as much dynamite as he needed to do the job! At any rate, I spent a sleepless night, for I was losing confidence in everything by that time—the two men, their rig, and my own luck. The suspense had been very long.

Next morning they did come back, as promised, and had everything ready to go in a surprisingly short time. I came out and stood at a little distance to watch. If the house was going to be blown up, I might as well try to stay alive!

The blast, when it came, was terrific. It took some seconds for the smoke to clear, and when it did I saw before me a slimy, mud-covered house instead of a white one . . . from sills to roof it was solid black! This was not the last *straw*, it was an *avalanche*, and I howled my despair, frustration, and rage. There did seem to be some sheep's heads around. But at least they were kindly; the men promised to wash off the mud with a hose, once we had water, and we made a start right away with pails and rags.

When things get to a certain nadir of desperation, there is

nothing to do but laugh and make a fresh start. It was a relief to go at those black walls and windows and put in a stiff few hours of sheer physical effort. It cleared out some of the piled-up anxiety, and I found comfort in the plain fact that things could not now get any worse.

It was almost a pleasure to hear the thud and knock, thud and knock, start up again; at least we had got through the boulder. The first part of drilling for water means getting down through layers of mud, gravel, and sand to the hard rock, to the ledges where artesian water may flow. Every day I had asked, "Are you near the ledges?" and every day I was told, "Not yet." By now, four weeks after the nightmare had begun, I expected it to go on forever. So I was taken wholly by surprise when the boss rapped sharply at the door and I saw his cherubic face beaming.

"We've hit it!"

"The ledges?"

"The ledges *and* water! Look at that . . ." and he pointed at a black torrent racing down the road.

"Are you sure?" I asked, unbelieving.

"Well, it's water, that's sure. We still have to see how much you'll get."

It was thick and muddy, but it was water, and would clear out if we ran it long enough, five gallons a minute he figured after measuring the flow. And we had hit it at only eighty-six feet! This was better than my wildest hope. (Miss Morrison had had to go to four hundred, and even Perley only reached the source at one hundred and forty.)

Just before mailtime I was watching for Win French so I could share my good news right away, and when I saw the station wagon streak past, I pulled on my boots and ran to meet him at the row of mailboxes on the village green. He stuffed a pile of letters into my hands, and we stood there for a few minutes talking, while I had no idea that what I held in my hands that unforgettable day, January 13th, 1965, was a staggering shift in the gambler's luck. It had been a long bad streak. When

I got back to the house, the first letter I opened told me that my editor at W. W. Norton's was delighted with *Mrs. Stevens*, that they would publish, and how would I like the advance? I had hardly taken in this amazing news when I opened another letter. It held the offer of a job as Poet in Residence at Lindenwood College, at a salary better than Wellesley had paid. I felt quite dizzy with joy, and so tired, suddenly, that I lay down and slept, as I remember it, for two hours. Then, still dazed, and a little shaky, I telephoned Judy in New Brunswick, where she was teaching that year, and, with her joyous response in my ears, I began to accept that all this good news was real.

As I look back, now, on the whole sequence of that bad time, I have no regrets. We have to make myths of our lives; it is the only way to live them without despair. This is not to dramatize so much as to look for and come to understand the metaphor that reality always holds in it. The inner world, the world of poetry, is as much nourished by the bad times as by anything. What I felt when all the good news came, in one huge bundle, on January 13th, was *relief:* I was over the hump. But what I had felt when I got back to poetry at Yaddo, during the very worst time of all, was *joy.*

I do not believe I shall ever again experience the panic I lived through at Yaddo. When water flowed up at five gallons a minute out of all that anxiety and despair, it suggested that if one can go deep enough, one will come to rock. By the end of the bad time, I had learned a lot about water, and where and how it is found.

THIRTEEN

Guests and Ghosts

I OFTEN FEEL that my guests here at Nelson become ghosts after their departure, good haunters, so great is the reverberation of every presence in the solitude; and in the same way, the ghosts I found here when I first came are guests. After eight years the house hums with memories, feels like a snug hive. Anyone who has stayed here for more than a day has helped to make the honey. And of course I inherited a store from those who lived here before me. If the oriole hunts for that branch of a maple which is no longer there, do the ghosts of Dr. Rand's horses sometimes give a long whiffle where the old barn stood? At any rate I have come to think of Aunt Cora Tolman as an old friend; I think of her when I am dusting and of her phrase "chickens" about those fluffy cocoons of dust one finds under a bed some-

Photograph by the author

times. I know from what Mildred has told me that she had a
particular way of seeing and of saying things—"I must be up by
sparrow-fart," for instance. Now and then someone turns up in
Nelson who remembers her vividly and her way with children;
one man had not forgotten a cookie jar filled with delicious
cookies, when he sat in my kitchen twenty years later and talked
about "Aunt Cora" with something like awe.

There is no doubt that she had an aura. Was it partly because of her infirmity? For she was a hunchback, and the hunchback has always been treated—not only in fairy tales—as in
some way both cursed and blessed. Was it because of her passionate love of flowers? Everyone who speaks of her always as-
sociates her with tending a garden, even when she was ill. Was
it partly because she had a very hard life but surmounted it?
Her second marriage was not easy, because her husband, who
farmed the place for her, liked to drink, and sometimes became
violent when he had a little more than he could hold with equa-
nimity. The ghosts in the house are not all sweetness and light, I
am glad to say, or I should not feel at home here as I do. After
"Aunt Cora" died, Quig painted several portraits of her. In one,
the gaunt, intense face looks out, a little incongruous above the
white dress; the deep-set eyes are very blue. It is a New England
face *au pur*. But in the white dress and in the softness of the
background, there is an added gentleness, a mystery. By means
of them I am sure the painter hoped to capture something of the
"aura" of the woman, something more than courage or fortitude,
a little touch of magic.

"Move but a stone and start a wing" . . . I cannot lift a
book down from the shelves in my study, or step from one room
to another, without starting up a silent commotion—the life that
flows through the house because of all that has been gathered
here and goes on growing as I grow.

I have known from the beginning that the true presence of the
house can be felt only when one is alone here, so I like to lend it
to a friend when I myself am absent . . . only then can a guest
have any idea what life here is like, and what the silences of

Nelson hold.

I sowed the first garden—that time it was hard to leave it—for a friend who came to be here and look after the cat while Judy and I spent some weeks in Europe. Kathryn Martin began her first novel sitting at my desk. As I evoke her and those long mornings of concentrated effort, broken by a visit to the garden so that she could tell me the shirley poppies were in flower, or that the bluebird had come back, or that the phoebes were building, I see Union Suit's sweet face, his large green eyes looking down from the window at the peak of the barn, like a small white owl. He liked to sleep in the hay, and waited there in the window to be called in for his supper. His ghost is still there.

For Kathryn Martin the month here was a coming back to the green of her childhood New England from the bare hills of California, where she was teaching at that time. She loved the solitude. "One hears voices but they have been there all the time," she wrote.

For Gunther and Rose Neufeld, who followed her that first summer to be keepers of the cat and the solitude, it was a coming home to Europe, for they had been refugees from Hitler, and no one has lived here who has been more aware of the ways in which New England and Europe are intertwined in these rooms. Here in my study Gunther meditated one of his explorations of the genesis of an Italian painting of the Renaissance. Each guest brings his own world with him and leaves a little of it with me afterwards. The Neufelds did much wandering in the woods, and not only told me of the unsuspected riches they held in the shape of edible mushrooms, as well as wild flowers, but welcomed me home with an exquisite tiny garden in a bowl, containing moss, a brilliant yellow-and-white mushroom, and a pair of silvery Indian pipes.

Each guest enriches the atmosphere with his own work, so the ghost of Chaucer was here for a few days while Helen Corsa was deep in her book on his "Mirthful morality," and after she left I entered for the first time into a dialogue with Chaucer, whom I had, in my ignorance, hardly known. How often, as I sit here at my desk, looking out through the hall to the cosy room, I evoke the exquisite, slender presence of Ellen Douglass Leyburn lying on the couch there reading Henry James . . . she is one of the presences who has come, but will never come again, for she has since died, leaving behind her as a legacy of her distinguished and original mind the book she was meditating on her last visit to Nelson.

I had hoped that this house might prove a haven for the anthropologist Cora Du Bois. She had been much in my thoughts when I first decided to buy, for she is one of the few people I have known who really enjoys hard outdoor work and the combination Nelson offers of concentrated hours of study with endless happy chores in the garden. It happened, however, that shortly after I came here, she embarked on a project that takes her to India nearly every year, so Nelson will have to wait. Nevertheless in the two or three weekends she has spent here, she has taken her place in the hive, and her presence is all around me, in the charming small painting of Ganesh, the Elephant God, which hangs just behind me in the study, in a set of soufflé dishes in the kitchen (for Cora is a great cook), and in innumerable useful and beautiful objects all over the house. And on one weekend she accomplished a heroic piece of digging, to open up a new flower bed under a low stone wall. The site turned out to have been a burying ground for all sorts of rubbish, so by the end of the morning Cora had unearthed not only the usual rocks but rusty tins, old nails, and broken china galore! Will she come back one day to see what that morning's work made possible? In late June that bed is a splendor of delphinium and lilies.

Lately the person who comes and goes while I am away is Eleanor Blair, who not only is a far more careful and efficient weeder than I, but has brought a new art and a new skill to the place by taking wonderful photographs of Perley Cole with his scythe, of lacy flowers against a granite boulder, of the triumphant brook tumbling out through the snow in spring, and who has held forever one of my huge, ephemeral bunches of flowers in her lens.

The guests are not all human ones. I never know what face may suddenly come out of the woods and for a moment stop to look at me in perfect innocence. One afternoon I glanced up from the sink, where I was washing dishes, and saw a superb young buck, his horns still covered in velvet, standing under the apple tree by the barn, an apparition so thrilling and unexpected that it took on the power of a dream. I took off my shoes and crept out on bare feet through the grass to look long at this living splendor, who wagged one ear, then stood absolutely still and unafraid, his liquid eyes fixed on mine. I was within ten feet of him and could see the light through the veined ears, when he gave a little huff, turned quite slowly, flashed his white tail, and bounded away in long easy bounds.

Sometimes a guest may cause hilarity. One winter day two flying squirrels discovered the wild raspberry bushes and played for an hour like trapeze artists, their white stomachs flashing as they swung from branch to branch to capture the infinitesimal dry seeds still hanging there. I haven't laughed with sheer joy like that since a pair of speckled cats, the successors to Union Suit, chased fireflies in the long grass when they were kittens.

Occasionally a human guest appears uninvited to bring an unexpected joy to the house. Only the other day, in the middle of a snowstorm, a young girl drove up at dusk, on her way north, long hair flying, and bearing in her arms a 'cello in its case. After I had lit the fire and made tea, she offered to play for me. A 'cello in the hands of a young girl is rather like some magic animal, to be cozened and caressed into uttering its rich haunting voice. That voice is now one of the good ghosts of the house, so much more alive than even the greatest record could be, even to the slight roughness of the bow against the strings.

I am not really a good host (except when I am absent myself), because even the dearest and long-expected guest is an interruption to the extended meditations of my deepest life here. That is why animals are in many ways the most welcome guests of Nelson; they go about their lives while I go about mine. They demand so little! But even they are a responsibility in winter, when I may have to pull on boots and overcoat to refill the feeders as many as three times a day for flocks of screaming jays, gold-and-black evening grosbeaks, chickadees, several pairs of woodpeckers and nuthatches, and, a little later on, the raspberry-throated purple finches. It is troubling to realize that some of my guests are always in peril—that one may endanger them even by feeding, as I learned to my grief when I had tamed a raccoon last fall to come and get chocolate biscuits every night; he was killed by a neighbor who boasted of having shot six raccoons in October. Will that beautiful young buck be shot down when the hunting season opens again?

It is winter that brings on these anxieties. In summer, when the first hummingbird comes back, all anxieties fly away before his irresistible lightning energy, as he tastes each flower in the garden, flashing a ruby throat. Insured as he is by his speed, I can watch for him without that tightening of the chest as to how he will fare.

And now, since 1961, he brings with him, as surely as do the shirley poppies, the presence of Basil de Selincourt, whose visit had some of the resonance for me that Céline's had had. For Basil too was part of my life as a European. And he had been the great "friend of the work" since my first book of poems came out in England in 1939. (He had hailed it in a magnificent review in *The Observer*.) I had often been with him in his own garden near Oxford; he came to Nelson to see what I was doing with mine, and how the poet was faring in the country.

Basil resembled a wild bird, from the crest of white hair to the beaklike nose and piercing glance that noticed everything. When he came to Nelson he was in his eighties, and he came in the glow of triumph, for he had just planted and seen come to fruition a large vegetable garden in Tyrringham, where he was spending the summer. At eighty Basil's powers of sustained work out of doors were far greater than mine will ever be; he had the slow, unhurried walk of the real gardener—all in good time. He had long since given up being a professional critic. I think criticism imposed on him a tension very much like that imposed on the creator, but more painful because he had to deal with the work of others—and he was a man of extreme sensitivity as well as of ruthless honesty. In relation to me the literary critic had given way to the loving, contentious friend. No one has ever read my poems with more concentrated attention nor asked so much of me, but he stood *inside,* not *outside.* (His first wife had been Anne Douglas Sedgwick, and he was acutely aware of what it costs to be a woman and an artist.) Every writer needs one key person, one ear, one evaluator whom he can trust absolutely. There must be someone who registers triumphs with pure joy. Basil was that for me for more than twenty years.

There were other affinities. This most English of men was of French descent. Our blend was much the same blend, with, for each of us, the English side in the ascendant. Of course I had become ultra-American over the years, and my chauvinism caused an occasional rift; Basil could not admit equality either about race or education or even politics. He feared the dilution of excellence in the American way of life.

What he loved about this country was wild nature, the untamed quality, the vast uncultivated spaces of woodland and mountain in New England. He drank in the larger continental air. His was the most acute natural sensitivity I have ever known. He himself would have said that it stemmed less from cultivation or instinct than from denying himself any stimulant whatever except tea. He neither drank nor smoked, and regarded any excess in such matters with visible distaste. He wanted, I think, to remain as naked a man as possible within a civilized society, to keep his senses as acute as an Indian's. This physical purity had something to do, no doubt, with his kind of perception as a literary critic. His views had become, by 1961, unfashionable; I am unfashionable, too, and his criterion gave me strength to go my way against the tide. Let me cite one example of it, from a letter.

"I can't quite agree about the use of the term 'violence' in connection with creative art, even in the context supplied. No doubt, aboriginally, most intense feeling tended to express itself violently; but wherever there was love, the violence was for the warding off of externals, irrelevancies, dangers—and the core was tenderness—and surely the essentially creative element in art, as we now know it, is intensity of tenderness: for it is impossible to over-estimate the delicacy of touch, in every direction, demanded by loyalty to Truth."

This Basil came to Nelson, and what he found here of surpassing delight was the hummingbirds. During the two or three days he was here, while I worked he sat out in the garden behind the house and waited for the hummingbirds with a look of profound joy on his face, like a mage.

I made one bad mistake during those mornings: I am accustomed to playing records while I work. This non-listening or half-listening of mine to the genius of Mozart or Bach offended Basil so much that he gradually moved his bamboo chair farther out into the meadow, until he was both out of sight and out of sound. That was his way of doing things, and it contained a certain violence, the violence of the absolute. Unfortunately I imagined that he was moving because he wanted to be in those wilder parts of the garden, and realized too late that my use of music as a spur or as an opener of doors had seemed to him an outrage.

But when the hummingbird comes back in early summer, all conflict dies away and I remember only Basil's joy. It took many forms. When he was a very old man, past eighty, he who had been a critic became a poet. He even invented a form of his own, a twenty-two- or twenty-three-syllable poem. After he had left, he sent me one of these:

> T'have found the poet
> in a garden
> with hummingbirds—
> inextricable maze of light and love!

So I think I was forgiven.

It is in the character of this house to accrete delightful ghosts. One of them materialized, most unexpectedly, on December 19th, 1958, when Samuel Eliot Morison, in a letter to me, remembered: "Nelson! About fifty years ago, on a very cold April day, snow on the ground, I got lost riding horseback beyond Dublin and fetched up at Nelson. A kind farmer in a village house let me bait my horse in his barn and gave me milk and apple pie. Perhaps it is the very one you have now. So, add me to the house's ghosts—a very tired, bewildered, cold young boy on an even tireder gray horse—Blanco by name—fed and sent home (a good twenty miles) rested and happy."

How could I ever be lonely here?

FOURTEEN

The Turn of the Year

As THE YEAR and the seasons turn, there are only two occasions when we gather as a town, when the community, scattered up in the hills and around the lakes, comes together—old, young, farmers, professional men and women, poets and all. The first is our Town Meeting, the second Tuesday in March. Since March is apt to be more lionlike than lamblike around here, there may well be a blizzard on that day; I have seen several since I attended my first Town Meeting. If it is easy, then, for me to pull on boots and trudge a few hundred yards to the Town Hall across the green, how intrepid are those who must drive their jeeps, trucks, battered old cars, Mercedes Benzes, for miles through drifts and blinding snow to get there! I am always amazed at how many we are by the time Fran Tolman's gavel comes down.

Photograph by Eleanor Blair

Nelson Village, where I live, is only a small part of the Township of Nelson, which also includes Munsonville and Tolman Pond. Here in the village there is no business. Shops, post office, and gas station are all in Munsonville, two miles away on Granite Lake. But here, in the rural center, it all began, in the late 1700's, and here the Meeting House stands. It was brought down the hill from Packersfield (where the cemetery now is) in 1814, and rebuilt to celebrate the adoption of the new name and the new site. When the village had been incorporated in 1774 it had been agreed to name it for Thomas Packer in return for a promised three hundred acres, which never materialized. So when the move downhill took place, Mr. Packer was considered unworthy of the honor he had bought but never paid for, and the new name decided on was Nelson, in honor of the great Admiral. By that time the Hardy family had settled here. Did they remember Nelson's device, "Let him who merits bear the palm," and consider the name a subtle dig at Thomas Packer? At any rate we know that they were proud of a distant kinship with the immortal sailor, Hardy, to whom Nelson's last words, "Kiss me Hardy," had been addressed. So this town got its name because of a grudge and because of love, and from what I have known of it the singular combination is appropriate!

But whatever grudges may surface later on, Town Meeting begins as happy reunion. We have all been more or less snowed-in for months, and we are glad to have a chance to exchange the news; there is often a new baby to be admired or a newly married couple to be congratulated. Knots of old acquaintances gather in corners to prepare a strategy on some business ahead, or to boast of how many hedgehog noses they have brought in for bounty, or to ask "Did you get your deer?" There is a lot of friendly chaffing while late-comers look around for a spare seat on the hard benches, and the children gradually get sorted out and sit down. We of the Town sit in rows facing the platform where Fran Tolman, our Moderator for many years, will stand, with the Town Clerk at a table by his side.

When we are all finally unbundled and more or less settled,

Fran brings down his gavel—more than once, for it takes time to subdue the loud talk to a murmur—until at last he commands the attention of the whole gathering and can read aloud the twenty-five or more Articles in the Warrant that we are about to discuss and vote on. Some of us have attended a preliminary session when these matters could be discussed informally, questions asked, and the air cleared a bit where there might be controversy. All of us now have the printed Annual Report in our hands and can follow what Fran is reading aloud, although few of us do so. If there are any ticklish matters to come up, rumor has done its work, and sides have already been taken long before the Meeting. The Selectmen sit on the front bench, their backs to the rest of us, in comparative safety, at least for the time being.

I remember well how moved I was the first time I looked at the faces gathered there. They are an epitome of New England as things are now. No one, I think, could fail to be impressed by the character they show, especially the old faces—nor fail to wonder whether the children are being given the kind of life that creates such quality. We are dressed very much alike, all in boots, heavy coats, lumber jackets, woolen caps. At first sight there is apparent homogeneity. But under those coats and caps what differences in background and outlook! Among us there are millworkers who go over to the wool mill at Harrisville; there are teachers and professors; there is at least one preacher (a woman); there are two or three writers; there are carpenters, electricians, farmers, foresters, retired missionaries, businessmen, clerks, amateur gardeners, and there are the men whose job is our roads—the keeping of them open in winter and graded in summer. Occasionally a summer resident may come a long way to be present, but on the whole this meeting in March is composed of people who live and work here the year round. Hardly a piece of town business comes up which cannot be explained to the non-experts by an expert among us.

Perhaps this fine mixture of people is possible because industry in this vicinity has remained a matter of small factories—

often, as in the case of Harrisville, a family affair where each workman is known as friend and neighbor. We are a highly diversified society because there is no one easy way to make a living, and because we are still a society with roots in the land itself, however barren the land may be.

Because we do represent a variety of points of view and character, the Town Meeting at Nelson is explosively human. So it is more than usually important to have an experienced moderator, as Fran Tolman is. We benefit from his procedural knowledge, gained as Clerk of the House in Concord, from his long experience of our specific problems here as landowner, expert hunter and fisherman, and from his sensitivity as a human being. We can trust him to be fair about whom he "recognizes," and to know when the time is ripe to close the discussion without hurt feelings. Much has been written about "grass roots" democracy, usually of a glowing and romantic kind. I have learned a lot in these few years of attending the Nelson Town Meeting, and it is not all glowing or romantic. Some of it has made me think hard. Even in such a small town as this we vote huge sums of money with very little discussion—for a new grader, for instance, which may cost $20,000. The real haggling seems to be over very small sums. This year the longest discussion took place on whether to raise the policeman and the constable from $15 a year to $50! Is this, I wonder, because, on a comparatively small issue, we feel more competent to judge? I have come to feel that a democracy asks more of each of us than we have been trained to give, or are willing to give. We should know more than we do, even in this small town, about what we vote on, whether it be schools, cemeteries, road equipment, or a new fire truck. Our votes are too often based on mere hunches, grudges, or irrational faith in one proponent as against another. They are too often based on propinquity: Munsonville is apt to vote against Tolman Pond, for instance, because the Pond is across two or three hills in a different world. The people who speak to the point, and from knowledge, are few, and some of the most knowledgeable do not speak at all. Prejudice plays its part. Too often we prove ourselves inadequate to the task before us, that of ruling a small community with wisdom and justice.

Some years ago a bitter battle was fought over hard-topping a piece of steep hill-road that abuts on the village green. The road agent and those on his side of the argument believed the dirt road presented a serious hazard at mud season, when it becomes less a road than a muddy river that dumps itself in Mildred Quigley's garden. Mud season is the time when burials take place of all those who have died during the winter, and one old lady vividly described the hearses getting stuck on their way to the cemetery, a harrowing sight. The question before us was whether to hard-top a few hundred feet of the steep incline. The opposition group, some of whom have horses and depend on keeping as many dirt roads as possible for riding, were dismayed at what hard-top would do to the early-American look of the village green. They feared, too, that if the hard-topping of these lovely country roads once began, it would never end. They and most of the summer people were fighting to keep the "sweet especial rural scene," but in this instance at the price of convenience and neighborliness. The whole business came close to being a feud. It even got into the local papers, which did not help.

At Town Meeting that year the hard-top question was discussed with fury. Several citizens brought prepared speeches; others leapt to their feet to make angry answers. Fran Tolman had to exert all his charm and skill to keep the peace. I was among the passionate myself. But I learned something that day. I learned the amazing effect, after so much emotion, of the cold, hard counting of votes. Everyone had had his say, and when the ballots were in, calm followed on the storm. People who, a few moments before, had flushed red with anger, smiled again, even when their side had proved to be the losing one. This is a small instance of how the democratic way shows its true strength. And I shall not forget it. It is Anglo-Saxon. I sense this with my Belgian self, for in Belgium, as in France, where political passions run high, what is often missing is that calm after the storm, the kind of generosity that can yield gracefully and without bitterness to the wishes of a majority.

This is one of the things I see on the deeply lined yet gentle faces around me in Nelson—a saving sense of humor, an essential good will toward each other, possible here, perhaps, because we can still know each other as individuals and accept each other's eccentricities as part of what makes life interesting. Passions there are bound to be in every small community. I sometimes think people have to have a grudge to keep them warm in winter!

But these grudges tend to unknot themselves as the warm weather comes, and by the time the next gathering of the whole town takes place, Old Home Day, on the second Saturday of August, they have slipped away with the snow and the bitter winter winds, and we are in harmony again, a community that for over two hundred years has evoked deep love in its members.

One of them, a legendary bachelor of means, embraced the village with such affection that it is said of him, "Nelson was his bride." To him we owe the splendid brass tablet on the Meeting House wall which names the one hundred and twenty-three men "who, as volunteers, answered the call to arms, for the preservation of the Union," and celebrates them with quotations from Lincoln, Bret Harte, and Lowell. To that same fervent bachelor we owe the great stone monument in the cemetery that commemorates the War of Independence and lists the amazing number who left their families and farms unprotected and rode off to Lexington and Boston. There is a bench in that green and quiet place where I often sit to ponder those names.

Not all of Nelson's lovers can afford such munificent gifts, but to the memory of one other we owe the Lydia Rodham Memorial Library across the green from my house—the smallest and neatest library I have ever seen, a library which might have been attended by Peter Rabbit himself!

If, at Town Meeting, we wrangle about the immediate future, on Old Home Day we gather in love and rejoicing to celebrate a long and glorious past. It is August and we can usually count on fair weather, which is just as well because people will be coming from far and wide; everyone who has ever been connected with the town is invited. Fifty years ago the Hardy family drove over from Vermont in a big wagon with a team of horses, spent the night in Marlborough, and then came on to take over my house, which they then owned, for the day. Part of the adventure for the children was opening up the closed house, and dusting and sweeping while their mother laid newspapers down on the kitchen table and spread out food there; for them it was "playing house" in a real house. And for them even the long drive home was part of the fun. They still remember walking up the steep hills to give the horses a rest, and singing hymns in the dark on the last lap to keep their spirits up. Now two of the Hardy sisters can just step out from the parsonage to greet their friends on Old Home Day, and others of the clan are within a few minutes drive. But every summer someone from far away manages to come back to renew old acquaintance and to sign the book kept open on a table under the trees in front of the church, recording there, one more name among so many others, the magnetism this small village exerts, and has exerted for two hundred years.

I don't suppose I shall ever recapture quite the sensation Old Home Day gave me the first time I was part of it. It was so unlike anything I had ever seen! For days before, I had been aware that everyone who lives near the green was sprucing up—lawns were being carefully mowed and trimmed; the church was swept; the granite posts around the Civil War monument, which always get knocked down by the plows in winter, were set straight again. Then on the Friday, a truck turned in bearing the speaker's stand, which was carried out, canvas roof, lectern and all, to be placed at the bottom of the slopes facing the church; the microphone was tested and re-tested. I was kept pretty busy keeping track of all this and sprucing up myself. Our placid, green world had come alive.

Early on the day itself, trestle tables appeared under the

maples just beyond the church, and the materials for a barbecue on the green, as well as several large logs—I did wonder about them! By eleven o'clock, the village, usually so empty and tranquil that it seems to be lost in dream, was the scene of great animation. Children and dogs were running about; two or three ponies were being led across the green. Cars drove up and emptied out people of all ages. A bus drew up to unload a remarkable band, none of whose members, men or women—yes, there were women among them—could have been under sixty. They made a splendid sight, lugging their trumpets, trombones, xylophones, drums, and camp stools, the men in shirt sleeves and straw hats, the women in summer dresses, so they looked more like a large family than an official band. They settled themselves slowly, opening up instruments and setting up music stands, in a double semicircle under a big maple to the left of the church and below it. With the church's gothic façade as back wall, and the orchestra and speaker's stands as stage, the lawn had now become a theater where the audience was already beginning to gather in "orchestra seats"—the long benches which provided a vantage point for all that was happening.

I had been watching from the house, a little shy of going out alone into this strange new world. But by now the loudspeaker was sounding quite imperative, and I felt compelled to join the crowd. I wandered out, stopped a moment to watch the men pitching horseshoes in the sand by the side of the road along my meadow, then moved into the center of things on the green. Those big logs that had puzzled me were now set up on trestles; and two of the older boys were busy organizing a sawing contest. Meanwhile twenty or more of the smaller children had engaged in an epic tug of war, pulling first one way, then the other, in short bursts of energy, until one side fell down with screams of laughter. Other children scrambled for pennies in a sawdust heap, and still others had been lured by a round target set up in my meadow and were engaged in shooting with bows and arrows. Two little boys scrambled up and down a rope hung on the strong branch of a maple. The parents tended to congregate in front of the church, lugging picnic baskets up to "save a place" at one of the trestle tables, and clustering here and there to talk. The inhabitants of the town are scattered so far from each other that Old Home Day is a rare chance to get together. The band had begun to tune up; an occasional grunt or bellow came from the big brasses.

It was all rather wonderful to me, so casual yet so orderly, so well organized for individual pleasures, and these pleasures such simple ones. I loved it—why, everything that was being done with such gusto around me might have been going on a hundred years ago! That was the key to it all, to the charm. Yet there was nothing self-consciously "old-fashioned" about all this. It was just a big, informal, family picnic where games are improvised out of whatever is handy—a rope, a log, a few pennies, or whatever. Only the band had a professional air—we vote a definite sum in March at Town Meeting to pay for it—and was indeed a group of musicians who took themselves seriously, and who tootled, blew, and thumped out every familiar "piece," from the Sousa marches to "The Last Rose of Summer," with serene unself-consciousness. If I found them endearing, it was because they too had remained such individuals; they had none of the false sheen of snappy uniforms and drum majorettes. They were a good old-fashioned band, and they knew it.

The games take place before lunch, but as at any good picnic everything is going on at the same time and no one gets hurried or flustered. Those of us who have houses on the green usually invite our guests to eat outside on our own lawns, so there are tables and deck chairs set up all over the village, and small groups gather under the trees, opening baskets and spreading cloths, while the more elderly tend to congregate at the comfortable trestle tables beside the church. Trees, people in bright summer colors, green lawns . . . it is a lovely sight.

After the picnic baskets have been gathered up, at somewhere around two o'clock (this is a timeless day), the serious part of the festivity begins. By then people are moving toward the church, some to rest on the benches there, some to lie on rugs on the grass, a few to sit on the stone steps in the sun, while "the band plays on." That first year I walked around drinking in the charm of these casual groups under the trees, enjoying the feel of the village come alive in just this way for just this day, reluctant to take my place and give up the pleasure of looking on at the whole scene as it shifted to make new centers and shapes under the sharp thrust of the steeple against the blue sky. . . . But someone was adjusting the microphone; it was time to settle down before the speech began.

At last the late-comers settled in, the benches were full; a little girl ran to her mother's arms; the murmurs and laughter died down, and our minister gave the prayer of invocation. The speaker was introduced and rose to celebrate the occasion, as such speakers do, with rather long-winded reminders of what makes New England memorable, and dear Nelson especially so.

It is pleasant to sit still after all the running about, and to be gathered together in silence for a change. I find the Old Home Day speech rather like going to church when I was a child . . . I dreaded having to sit still for so long, yet afterwards I was glad that I had been forced to do so. It is an act of communion, and even when the sermon is dull something does happen deep inside because one has participated in an act of communion. After the speech, the band launches into its real program, and most of us sit or lie around looking up at the leaves, and at the children playing on the green, and across to the tiny library on the hillside, in great contentment of mind. We have talked and listened ourselves out.

By the time the band has soared to its last brave climax of trumpets, trombones, and drums, the barbecuers are busy spreading out chicken on the long iron grids. On that first Old Home Day for me, I went home to supper, and to welcome one or two acquaintances who sauntered over to see my house (after all, it had changed a good deal since Old Home Day the year before), and to think over the long rich day.

But it was not yet over, as I had imagined it might be. After supper there is a square dance in the same hall where we have Town Meeting. I walked over after dark to peep in, and to sit for a while on the benches at the side of the room with others who had come, like me, to watch. Some of the best and fleetest dancers, I noticed, were well into their sixties. Quig was there that first year, with his violin tucked under his chin. Lately Newt Tolman brings his flute to help out the small orchestra, which makes up in verve for what it lacks in numbers.

That night I lay in bed, reliving the whole wonderful day and thinking it had been unique, unlike any experience I had ever had. But then a curious comparison rose in my mind as I remembered those days in Santa Fe when Haniel Long and Alice and I had packed a picnic basket and driven thirty miles or so to the Corn Dance at San Ildefonso. There too, among the Indians of the pueblos, all is apparently casual and relaxed; dogs and small children may run across the plaza while the gravest of dances is in progress; the "devoutness," as Haniel called it, is taken with ease; the rite brings together a whole community, young and old, as participators . . . yes, there is a similarity. As a community we are less religious; we no longer share in any religious rite that pulls in everyone, nor do we ask of ourselves the long meditations that the Pueblo dancers impose on themselves. But we do come together, in this town, every year, on Old Home Day, with something like devotion. It is not spoken aloud. It is hidden under the chaffing and the children's shouts. But it is there. I felt it on that first Old Home Day—the invisible structure of belief that holds us together and makes us a family at heart.

But belief in what? I asked myself that night. Perhaps it should be called a hope rather than a belief—the hope that while so much has changed, and will change, in our highly accelerated society, a few values can be maintained that have come to us from the past, that we may remain a town where the eccentric finds shelter, the original mind flourishes and is sustained, and the children are brought up to love these hills and brooks and woods as passionately as their grandfathers did. For is it not the love of the wild places that binds us all together—foreigners like me, summer people, and those who pride themselves on being natives?

Only the other day our road agent told me he had been offered a great deal more money than he can ever earn here, but the job would have meant a move into suburbia. "I could never stand it," he said, shaking his head, and looking, as he always does, near exhaustion. He would rather drive a snowplow all night, set up a lumber mill on his brook, do a hundred different odd jobs, and be able to give his children ponies to ride and a baby skunk to tame, and to have dogs running around loose, than to be "secure" in a row of identical houses. I can see his point.

Town Meeting and Old Home Day are public rites; there is one more rite, a private one, that has also become part of the seasonal rhythm of Nelson for me. It is the day, sometimes early in August, sometimes as late as September, when the Warners come to cut the hay in my big meadow. The Warners are the only family group among us who still run a farm, although Mr. Warner Senior also works on the state roads. Bud, the oldest son, and his sister Helen are the real farmers of the clan. They have a herd of cows and three or four horses to help with heavy work. Grace Warner, their mother, puts in a huge vegetable garden. Sally is the cook and has two or three flower beds to care for. Gracie takes care of rabbits, ducks, guinea pigs, goats, a pet sheep or two, two ponies, and a magnificent donkey called Esmeralda. Married sons cluster at the foot of the hill, staying close to the family farm. It remains a small truly rural corner in a township that has almost ceased to be farming country, and as such it is precious.

When I feel the need of a change I drive up a series of steep hills to that secret eyrie of theirs to see what is going on, for the Warners, struggling hard to keep afloat, are in the middle of a thousand adventures every day. It may be that a porcupine has climbed high up into an elm and eaten the bark off all the top branches; it may be that a litter of baby rabbits has been born, or a new calf; it may be that the iris is in flower in the pond where muscovy ducks and white geese paddle about so happily; it may be that Sally's sweetpeas are out—there is always something for Gracie to show me in this "Farm of Contented Animals," as it is so aptly named.

The Warners help me just by being there. When I went through that very hard time in 1964, in the middle of the drought, when every door seemed closed against me, Grace Warner telephoned one day across the hills to say, "We're all rooting for you!" It was wonderfully heartening.

And how often I have taken heart, after sitting for a few minutes in the tiny kitchen in that dilapidated old house which has, over the years, seemed to sink deeper into the earth, as if it were becoming a part of the natural world. Here in the kitchen the life of the house gathers at mealtimes, and here one is *inside* "the peaceable kingdom"—a litter of kittens under the stove, one or two dogs under the table, a single goldfish swimming around in a bowl on a shelf, a cage of birds hanging from the ceiling, and always a baby being fed on someone's lap. There I ask my foolish questions and receive sensible answers. On one of my first visits, I remember, I inquired whether they could spare a few bushels of manure. I caught the look of amusement on their faces, and understood why when Bud took me out and showed me a mountain of manure almost as high as the barn it lay against—a few bushels indeed!

Bud and Helen are kept pretty busy all summer, not only on their farm but cutting hay for a dozen or more neighbors and summer people, so I have to take them when I can get them. I am willing to wait, even as late as September, because I hate to see the black-eyed Susans and asters go. On the other hand, I love the familiar rite because while it is happening, for two or three days, my own place looks like the real farm it once was, and is no longer.

The day begins with the arrival, as like as not, of Gracie riding one of the big work horses bareback, with one or two small children behind her on his fat rump. She is followed by Bud and

Helen in the old truck, hauling the hay rake behind them. Doris rides the other work horse down, attracting in her wake four or five children, like a Pied Piper. I have pails of water ready for the horses, but that is as far as my duties go. Then, for three days, the big meadow is alive, and while the Warners work hard around me, I work the better for this brave company.

But I try to be there to watch when Bud leads the two great horses out to cut the first swathe in the long grasses, and what has been a rich diversity of nodding plumes turns over in a long green wave behind him—his way with the work has so much gentle style. This year there is a new horse in the pair, and dear old Chubby stands sedately in the barn at home. He went blind long ago, but so expert were Bud's hands on the reins that no one could have known it, watching the team go down the field as if to an inner music. Chubby's blindness could be managed, but in the last years he had begun to have "spells" and some-times nearly fell. I have seen Doris lean her full weight against him to keep him upright, and it was a pretty tense second when I wondered if I should see the huge horse fall on top of that tiny, intrepid person. No Warner would work a horse too hard; they kept him going for his own pleasure, not for theirs, and no doubt he is bored in his stall these days. But it was a relief to hear, last summer, that that ordeal was over and that a new horse, Molly, had taken her place on the team beside Dick.

My meadow gets harder to cut every year because brush and the ubiquitous alder are growing up around the rocks, and the grass itself is getting thinner. It must be kept down; it is the open space that gives the whole view its dimension. And, much as I love the wild flowers and hate to see them go, it is always a pleasure to watch my small "estate" emerge once more from jungle. I realize then that I had begun to feel a bit crowded in by the lush August growth on every side and its massive greens. The pale gold expanse before me changes and opens out the whole landscape, and frames the thin line of hills at the horizon, as if the trimmed field had become a greatly expanded lawn.

But we still have two or three days to go before the job is

completed. When Bud has finished—and that means, these days, a lot of scything where the mower can't reach—Doris appears on the hay rake, an elegant slim figure driving a single horse, her cap of red hair flashing in the sunlight. They have quite an air, those two—horse and driver. This last stage of the work takes in the whole family as everyone sets to, throwing forkfuls of hay up onto the battered old truck until it is bulging on every side, and lumbers up to the barn door like some ancient animal itself, with a covey of kids on its back.

I inherited the Warners and the haying, for they had been accustomed to cut and store the hay from my meadow in the barn before I bought the place, and I was only too glad to keep tradition going. Sometime in February, when hay is getting scarce, they will come down and get this extra supply and take it home to help keep all those animals contented. Until then I have the pleasure of getting a sweet whiff of summer when I open my barn door in below-zero weather.

So, just as Old Home Day and Town Meeting do, the Warner clan keeps alive in the village things that have deep roots in the past, those rites which are also renewals.

FIFTEEN

Plant Dreaming Deep

IT WAS FIVE YEARS before the plum trees I had planted flowered, five years before the oriole came back to weave his flame in and out of the clusters of white. I shall soon have been planted here myself for ten years, and I have a sense that the real flowering is still to come, and all I have experienced so far only a beginning. I have touched only the surface of the silences of Nelson; they will take me deeper and deeper, I hope, to their own source, as I grow older.

"*Nous arrivons tout nouveaux aux divers âges de la vie . . .*" I used La Rochefoucauld's wise saying as the epigraph for a novel some years ago. Then I recognized its wisdom, but had not yet experienced it for myself. Now the adventure before me seizes me in the night and keeps me awake sometimes. Growing

Photograph by Eleanor Blair

old . . . why, in this civilization, do we treat it as a disaster, valuing as we do the woman who "stays young"? Why "stay young" when adventure lies in change and growth?

It is only past the meridian of fifty that one can believe that the universal sentence of death applies to oneself. At twenty we are immortal; at fifty we are too caught up in life to think much about the end, but from about fifty-five on the inmost quality of life changes because of this knowledge. Time is suddenly telescoped. Life in and for itself becomes more precious than it ever could have been earlier . . . it is imperative to taste it, to savor it, every day and every hour, and that means to cut out waste, to be acutely aware of the relevant and of the irrelevant. There are late joys just as there are early joys. Young, who has time to look at the light shine through a shirley poppy? The outer world is only an immense resonance for one's own feelings. But in middle age, afternoon light marbling a white wall may take on the quality of revelation.

There is another subtle change: we become contemporaries, or nearly, of people who used to seem much older. Former teachers become friends; they, who seemed long ago when we were children to live on some Olympus light years away, are suddenly very close to us in actual age. We communicate at last as equals, and this is a new kind of delight. As we begin to catch up with them, we begin to understand a great deal about the dead that we could not know when we were young and they were old. When I first knew Jean Dominique, she was about my age and I was twenty-five. I have caught up with her, and our communion is thereby deepened. So, although time is telescoped in some ways, in others it mysteriously opens out; we have become infinitely more inclusive and extensive than we could ever be when young.

At the same time—and this is really the greatest richness of middle age—we are more and more available and to be depended on by the young. When I was twenty I knew what a word could mean from a writer I trusted, what manna from Heaven the support of a Basil de Selincourt, the generous interest of a Virginia Woolf or an Elizabeth Bowen! Praise for the middle-aged or old has always come too late; it cannot come too soon. Young talent thrives on it. How wonderful then occasionally to be able to give a lift up to a young poet whom one has admired! Is there another joy like this? It floods in to some perhaps still starved corner of the heart (for whoever got enough recognition when he was young?) and feels like fulfillment.

It is time to lay ambition and the world aside, and Nelson has been my way of learning to do just that. I have been so absorbed in making the garden that I have hardly noticed what was happening. There has been no act of renunciation, only the opening of a door into this new silence. And very subtly, in these last rich years what I value most has changed, for more and more I value the inward-turning of the life adventure.

That does not mean that friends become less precious; new ones appear like snowdrops through the snow, to be welcomed and cherished; old ones become dearer than ever because they help keep intact the delicate web of time, time past as well as time present. But old or new, they are seen in a different way now; loved less possessively, more for what they are, less for what we need from them. They are there, like the birds, to be rejoiced in as a part of the natural world on which our attention has come to be focused more intently than ever before, and more dispassionately. Or so it is for me at Nelson.

When I do see my friends here it is no longer for a conversation snatched at a lunch table in a restaurant, but for a leisurely visit. I am reminded on these occasions of the excitement children feel when a friend can be invited "to spend the night." Such a visit is prepared for with joy and wears a halo of time . . . time to make a special bunch of flowers for the guest room, time to cook a special meal, time to prepare the mind and heart.

I celebrated my fiftieth birthday with a last great journey, to see Japan, India, and Greece. I had the sense that it was then or never, that it would be harder and harder to leave my garden for an extended period, and that perhaps I would not again have

the gumption to get up and go off alone, at least not into exploring worlds strange and new to me. Who knows? The wanderlust
may seize me one of these days, but for the time being the most
intense experience seems to be right here.

For so long, ever since I was nine years old, Europe has
seemed the great haven, "the old nurse" as Eva Le Gallienne
once called it. Suddenly, last year, after a visit to old friends in
France, Belgium, and England, I felt an earthquake inside and
recognized one of those major shifts in consciousness which
mean that one has entered a new stage in life. I saw that the
time had come when I must become the old nurse myself, bring
my European friends here to America, to be cherished as they
had cherished me in Europe. So last autumn—and it turned out
to be a glorious one—I invited a dear friend from Belgium to
come and spend three weeks at Nelson. How wonderful it was
to be able to explain—at last without words—that the United
States is not only New York City, or the agony of Mississippi,
but also a village such as Nelson, intimate, quiet, and beautiful
—and almost empty! What joy to feel how astounding our
autumn color is to one used to the mellow melancholy of a Belgian October, to see my friend's eyes shine with excitement before my maples and asters! What joy to laugh with her at the fat
gray squirrels nibbling away on the snow under the bird feeder,
to sense her keen pleasure in this wilder landscape which, for a
European at least, still tastes of the frontier, to sit by the fire in
the big room in the evening and savor together the blue and
golden day already weaving itself into memory!

So the adventure opens out in all directions, even as it goes
deeper and comes from deeper. I feel in myself a greater power
to sustain extended periods of writing than I ever did before.
The long-distance runner may get tired, but he learns to breathe
a longer breath, and to hoard his strength for that last spurt.
Now, at fifty-five and past the meridian, I am setting my course
for a distant goal, am embarking on what may well take ten
years to finish, a project that will be accomplished here and have
to do with the New England ethos. For I do not mean that by

shutting out the world one resigns oneself to a passive "dwindling" into old age, as Millamant might have it. Quite the opposite . . . as I witnessed through my father, one cuts back to the essential, and in so doing releases explosive energies. My father wrote those two huge volumes on Greek and Hellenistic science after he had retired from Harvard and from teaching. And that vivid optimist had planned to write three or four or five more books—when he so suddenly and unexpectedly died in the midst of this vital flowering after seventy. Old writers do not fade away; they ripen.

What Nelson has given me is perhaps the ability to be a little more nonchalant about it all, a little less solemn and intense. We are all myth-makers about ourselves, but part of growing up, I suspect, is the shedding of one myth for another, as a snake sheds its skin. I have no illusions about my ever becoming a true countrywoman—there is too much behind me of a different kind. But it is a game, if you will, to superimpose the myth of the country person on the myth of the lonely battler for an old-fashioned style in poetry. I am sure one of the professional hazards the poet must face is the real danger of building up for himself the myth of the martyr, the solitary, unrecognized genius . . . well, we have to draw courage from somewhere. But I have observed that the genius-myth belongs to the very young. Those who insist on dressing up in it after fifty become slightly grotesque. By then one has survived, presumably. And one has settled for doing what one can, as well as one can, and taking the rest, so far as possible, as a joke on one's own pretensions.

What I am saying, I suppose, is that the romantic style or stance falls away, and one emerges from it more naked, more realistic, though no less vulnerable. I understand the sequence better for having observed it in microcosm in my relation to Nelson itself.

Here was a tangible reality outside myself, against which I could prove almost everything I have come to believe: the village, the house, the garden, the landscape all around have become for me one complex metaphor. Within the house I have proved to myself that my whole past, which I used sometimes to feel I was dragging behind me like one of those long tow sacks that cotton pickers drag behind them, can be integrated and function *as a whole.* The style of the house has been able to absorb all the varied styles of my European background, my wanderings and travels, and my various lives as an American. Here they all are at home—a collection of netsuke from Japan, paintings from India, Litvak's Lake Hopatoong, Quig's memory of Maine, the *bahut* from Belgium. And upstairs is a room containing nothing but files where the incredible accumulations of letters, papers, journals, and manuscripts are at last beginning to be sorted out and put in order—not only mine, but those of my father and mother.

Outside the house, the garden and the landscape beyond it bring together in focus a great variety of experience. The long herbaceous border evokes my mother's garden in Cambridge, and the smaller ones in front of the house are (symbolically) the flowery edges of a Flemish tapestry. Beyond them, since my return from Japan, the wilderness itself has taken on new meaning: the excrescences of rock in my meadow have become rare entities as if I lived in a huge Japanese rock garden.

Here the dead are not so much presences as part of the very fabric of my life; they are a living part of the whole. This way of absorbing death is not mourning. It does not look back romantically on the past; it builds the past into the present. So in a way I do not so much think about my father and mother as find myself in a hundred ways doing things as they would do. My mother tasted color as if it were food, and when I get that shiver of delight at a band of sun on the yellow floor in the big room, or put an olive-green pillow onto a dark-emerald corduroy couch, I am not so much thinking of her as being as she was.

When Katrine Greene, who died only last year, had, for a brief time, a remission and was outdoors in a wheelchair, she wrote me a paean of praise of life itself—a squirrel sitting up in the path to eat a nut, the raspberry-pink toes of a pigeon; and since her death I do not *try* to see such things with greater delight than ever before—it happens that I do. Katrine's bubbling laughter sometimes sounds through the house, as if she were sitting now on the little bench from River Houslin, back to the fire, her long legs stretched out, teasing me a little for taking life with too great solemnity. For what she is saying is, I think, "Let us live like Chinese philosophers, drunk on the moon."

I do not so much remember my father sitting those long hours bent over his desk answering letters, those letters that poured in on him from all over the world, those endless reprints from obscure assistant professors, to which he always responded —I do not remember so much as find myself driven by some compulsion stronger than memory, in the grain itself, always to answer any letter that comes to this house, and as soon as possible.

All of this has been the relation between me and what I brought here to Nelson. What of my relation to it?

When I first arrived, everything was an adventure, and it is that adventure that this book recounts. But already that exuberance, that time when I was in a perpetual state of wonder, curiosity, and sometimes dismay and fear, is changing. The romantic period of my life here is coming to a close.

I have learned now that not all New Englanders are reticent, honest, hard-working; we have among us the indifferent, the lazy, the cruel, as does any small community. Rural life intensifies the inner direction; it often makes for character at the expense of spontaneity and openness toward life. The provincial has his strengths, but he also has his peculiar narrowness. Tradition is a frame, but it can become a cage. The struggle for mere existence against the fiercely changeable climate takes something out of people. Sometimes life becomes thin in consequence. In the middle of winter one sees it in the faces, that unnatural pallor as of plants starved for sun and water. I do not love Nelson less for seeing what I now see. I take it as it is, as I try to take myself as I am and not worry over much or waste time in remorse for my own rages, tensions, and conflicts. These inner currents match the immensely variable currents of wind and rain and snow that make the New England weather more than a physical climate—a psychic climate.

Last summer an event took place which helped me to cast off the romantic phase of my relation to Nelson. The first I knew of it was the appearance, walking on the village green and lying about on the lawn in front of the church, of a group of young people in casual dress. Some carried instruments with them, or got out of cars holding the huge black bodies of 'cello cases or the small coffins that hold flutes and oboes. One of them, a tall young man with a full black beard, stood out as the leader. What were they up to? So little "happens" here that such an invasion was closely observed from the windows of the few houses that command the church, mine not excluded. When I went out for the mail, I heard unmistakable sounds coming from the church—not the tremulous vibrato of the organ played by Bessie Lyman's gentle hands, but a whole concord of instrumental voices—flutes and oboes and 'cellos and violins, and the plucked strings of a harpsichord. Surely Mozart was being played!

I went home, thoughtful, and waited for the matter to be explained. One thing is sure, we do not meddle in each other's business here, but sooner or later anyone's business becomes, by a kind of osmosis, public knowledge. So I did not have to wait many days before I knew what was happening. The Musica Viva Ensemble, as this group of young musicians called themselves, had been rehearsing in the neighborhood and looking for a hall or building acoustically viable for recording. They are a professional group—some of them had been at Tanglewood earlier on in the summer—composed of two flutes, two oboes, two clarinets, two bassoons, two French horns, four violins, a viola, a 'cello, a bass viol, and a harpsichordist. Their leader, James Bolle, had married a Keene girl, and thus the neighborhood of Keene was to be their region for the end of the summer. They had found the hall they needed in our church, had got permission to rehearse and record there, and in return offered us five concerts of Baroque music, much of it unrecorded until now. What a gift!

It was a beautiful dream. I could walk across the meadow as the full moon was rising, slip into a pew at the back of the church, and listen to this lively and musicianly group almost as if I and the village as a whole were the lords of a little duchy with a private orchestra to beguile the still summer nights. After the first concert (Bach and Haydn as I remember) I could not keep away, and more than once stole in late in the morning to listen to a rehearsal and to watch young Bolle at work. I am not a musician, but it is always a pleasure to look in on a true harmony in the process of creation. It reminded me of the long hours when I had sat in the dark at the Civic Repertory Theatre watching Miss Le Gallienne bring this harmony out of the company as they rehearsed a play of Ibsen's or of Chekhov's. I sensed in Bolle, as he stopped the musicians over and over to achieve perfection for one slight phrase, yet never lost his temper or his joy, the same genius for creating sufficient enthusiasm in the players to carry them over the endless repetitions, and even to enjoy themselves in the process. It takes a delicate human touch, as well as conviction.

Though the first concert had not been very well attended, word got around, and for the last four concerts the church was full or nearly full. During the intermission, players and audience sauntered out across the green to the old schoolhouse, where there is a kitchen, to drink coffee together out of paper cups. There we were, in the perfect stillness of the summer night, the great moon rising over the hill, the village itself luminously white, composed like a painting, and the human voices taking on that poignancy that a few voices take on under the stars surrounded by that immense silence.

As far as I was concerned this was pure delight—an unbelievable "happening." But I soon learned that some at least of my neighbors felt chiefly irritation. The orchestra, I heard it said, was a bunch of lazy beatniks; they made too much noise rehears-

ing—and who wanted to listen to eighteenth-century music anyway? Who did they think they were to take over the night when
hard-working people need sleep? Since I had not heard such
complaints of the often far noisier folk-dancing music in the
Town Hall, this made me stop and think. At that moment the
bubble of whatever romantic feeling I had had about Nelson
broke. The people who had crowded the church, I now realized,
were chiefly summer people; the true residents (though not all, I
must add) felt that all this had been simply an unwelcome in-
trusion! This was hard for me to take.

There is so much wisdom, so much kindness, so much sheer
knowledge among my neighbors that I had been for eight years
a learner among them. They had the key to much that I honored
and wanted to learn to share; now it dawned on me in a hard
cold light that I had a key to some things they lack. It had been
given to me, not earned—given by my parents, by my school, by
the Civic Repertory Theatre, by Jean Dominique, Basil de Selincourt, Virginia Woolf. I saw now that I had not been lonely in
Nelson because I am immune to loneliness, surrounded as I am
by such a cloud of radiance and belief. Nelson then has given
me the key to a natural world I knew next to nothing about
eight years ago; but it is not, and never can be, the key to all
that I treasure. It would be foolish to expect that it might be
. . . a foolishness common to lovers who expect *everything* of
the beloved!

Now as I play once more the record of Tommaso Albinoni's
Adagio in G Minor for Strings and Organ—the long grave
phrases that have accompanied me through much of the writing
of this book in praise of Nelson, I know that what lies ahead will
be richer than all that has gone before. For now I must go deep
not only into all that Nelson has to give but also into all that I
have still in me through this marriage of a wild natural world
and an ethos brought here from Europe.

Perhaps I can create what Jean Dominique asked of herself
in that moving final utterance:

Presse de ma douleur, O Maître,
Comme d'un pampre pur et vieux,
Le vin qui fait plaisir aux Dieux!

Who knows what that wine will be, or how John Elwes in his miserly extravagance, and Duvet de la Tour, the shrewd Norman, and all the others, the mysterious forefathers who have given me an atom of themselves to carry on through my father and my mother, will come to terms with this dear, provincial, rude, brave Nelson? All I know is that the responsibility is great; the wish, fervent; and that perhaps the makings are here to create a vintage wine for the delight of the gods.

May Sarton

POET, NOVELIST, TEACHER, she was born near Ghent, Belgium, and educated in the United States. She is the daughter of the Historian of Science, George Sarton.